50 GEMS
Gloucestershire

MARK TURNER

AMBERLEY

For Lucy

First published 2020

Amberley Publishing
The Hill, Stroud
Gloucestershire, GL5 4EP

www.amberley-books.com

Copyright © Mark Turner, 2020

Map contains Ordnance Survey data © Crown copyright and database right [2020]

British Library Cataloguing in Publication Data.
A catalogue record for this book is available from the British Library.

ISBN 978 1 4456 9740 6 (paperback)
ISBN 978 1 4456 9741 3 (ebook)

Typesetting by Aura Technology and Software Services, India.
Printed in Great Britain.

Contents

Introduction

Gloucestershire is predominantly rural in character, with even its two main population centres of Gloucester and Cheltenham being within easy striking distance of the Cotswold Hills and the Severn Vale's floodplain meadows. The county's geological diversity has resulted in the formation of three distinct regions, each with its own scenic characteristics. The gently rolling hills of the Cotswolds, dotted with picturesque towns and villages of honey-coloured limestone, perennially draw thousands of visitors, while the Forest of Dean, overlooking the Wye Valley and Welsh mountains beyond, has a somewhat dark and mysterious beauty quite distinct from the rest of Gloucestershire.

Flowing between these two regions is the mighty River Severn, which over countless centuries has carved a course through the land to create the Severn Vale. This is a low-lying area and, lacking an abundance of stone, builders commonly used timber frames in the construction of dwellings. Their work has produced numerous impressive houses, bearing characteristics much different to those of the neighbouring Cotswolds district. Many examples can be seen at towns and settlement areas along the route of the Severn, with Tewkesbury possessing a particularly striking collection. Paradoxically, however, some of Gloucestershire's most outstanding stone buildings – Gloucester Cathedral, Tewkesbury Abbey and Berkeley Castle – are found in the Vale area.

Contained within this topographically diverse county are many natural features of beauty and interest that might well be considered gems by many who see them. In addition to these features there are numerous buildings and structures of note. What is now known as Gloucestershire has received settlers over thousands of years – from the Neolithic period, through to the Bronze Age and Iron Age, following which the Romans invaded and occupied the country. Later still, of course, came the Norman invasion. These settlers and invaders brought their own cultures, going on to create many imposing and memorable features on the landscape. A number of these creations may justifiably be regarded as gems.

Somewhat contentious for inclusion, however, are the sites of conflicts or battles, remnants of industrial activity, or, perhaps, pubs and cafés. Clearly, one person's idea of a gem will not always find universal approval and to some degree, at least, the features included in this book are subjective choices. Some features simply *had* to be included – who, for example, would not consider Gloucester's magnificent cathedral a gem? Other choices are less obvious, but it is hoped that readers will be inspired to explore the county's gems and find at least some gem-like qualities in each place described.

Various people have been of assistance during my preparation of this book. I would like to give thanks and acknowledgement to Sean Bolan, Hugo Mander at Owlpen Manor, Jacqueline Newton and Benjamin Turner. Additionally, I wish to acknowledge the help and support from staff and volunteers at Batsford Arboretum, Hidcote Manor Gardens, Westonbirt Arboretum, Chedworth Roman Villa and Dr Jenner's House, Museum and Garden.

North Cotswolds

1. Cheltenham

Although the granting of a charter in 1226 established Cheltenham as a market town, it consisted at that time of little more than a long street and the Church of St Mary. The discovery of medicinal waters to the south of the town in 1716 brought about major change, however, and Cheltenham subsequently became a popular spa town. Infrastructure improvements followed in the 1780s, and, following a visit and holiday by George III and his family in 1788, the town's reputation as a fashionable resort was

Jazz Festival at Montpellier Gardens, Cheltenham.

Above: Municipal Offices at Cheltenham's Promenade.

Below: Pittville Pump Room, Cheltenham.

assured. Much building of attractive houses and terraces followed in the first half of the nineteenth century and, by the twentieth century, Cheltenham was well known as an upmarket shopping town and home to the prestigious annual Gold Cup horse race.

Among its fine Regency buildings, tree-lined Promenade and leafy parks, Cheltenham possesses numerous gems. A strikingly handsome terrace housing the Municipal Offices stands on the west side of the Promenade. Completed around 1835 and set back behind ornamental gardens, this great terrace is sixty-three bays long and stands three storeys high. The central bay is highlighted with four Ionic columns.

Montpellier, immediately south of the Promenade, is one of the most pleasing areas of the town. Among its inviting streets and terraces are various restaurants, wine bars and cafés, as well as a variety of individual and interesting shops. At the nearby Montpellier Gardens there is a bandstand of 1864, where concerts take place in the summer months. Imperial Gardens, with marvellous floral displays provided annually by some 25,000 bedding plants, are found to the rear of Cheltenham Town Hall.

The Town Hall and the nearby parks are the setting for Cheltenham's festivals – each one being a gem in itself. The Music Festival (formed in 1945), the Literature Festival (formed in 1949), the Jazz Festival (formed in 1996) and the Science Festival (formed in 2002) each host some of the biggest names in their field, attracting supporters and devotees from far and wide. Further information is available online at www.cheltenhamfestivals.com.

Pittville Park, which straddles Evesham Road to the north of the town, is Cheltenham's largest ornamental park. Opened in 1825, it forms part of the Pittville garden suburb, developed by wealthy banker and lawyer Joseph Pitt, and includes two lakes and the stately neo-Greek Pittville Pump Room among its features. Built between 1825 and 1830, and housing one of several wells opened in the town, the Pump Room building – which regularly hosts music concerts – has a domed roof and is surrounded by a colonnade of Ionic columns.

2. Northleach

The quiet town of Northleach, situated on the east side of the Roman Fosse Way, has not always been so tranquil. From the 1770s the main coaching road linking London and South Wales passed through the town centre, the constant presence of heavy traffic continuing until the construction of a bypass in the early 1980s. It was an important wool trading centre in the Middle Ages, by the fourteenth century exporting great quantities to Italy and the Low Countries, where merchants particularly prized wool from the Cotswolds.

The splendid Church of St Peter and St Paul, just above the Market Place, dominates the town. Among the greatest wool churches of the Cotswolds, and exemplifying the Perpendicular style of English Gothic architecture, much of it was built under the patronage of wealthy local wool merchant John Fortey. The tower, which dates probably to the late fourteenth century, was built first, the elegantly-pinnacled south porch and aisle being added in the early fifteenth century. The well-lit and loftily imposing nave followed in the mid to late fifteenth century. There is much of interest within the church, including the fourteenth-century font, fifteenth-century pulpit and a fine collection of monumental brasses to local wool merchants.

Standing at the junction of the High Street and Fosse Way is a building of exceptionally forbidding and austere appearance. It was built as a house of correction in 1789–91 by William Blackburn – a specialist in prison design – in accordance with a prison reform plan by Sir George Onesiphorus Paul, High Sheriff of Gloucestershire. Following Paul's death in 1820, however, conditions deteriorated at the prison with the introduction of hard labour, which included use of a treadmill. Prison welfare had improved by the 1850s and a police station and petty sessional court were incorporated into the building. In the 1930s the cell blocks were out of use, although the police and court services remained there until the 1970s. Today the former prison is a museum.

Northleach has on several occasions featured in television and movie productions. Part of BBC film *The Wyvern Mystery* (2000) was filmed in the town, while the Market Place featured prominently in British supernatural thriller movie *The Gathering* (2003). The Market Place appeared, also, in British-American Sky 1 series *You, Me and the Apocalypse* (2015). Northleach was used as the fictional town of Pagford for the BBC's adaption of J. K. Rowling's *The Casual Vacancy* (2015), with the town and its surrounding area appearing frequently in the BBC sitcom 'mockumentary' series *This Country*, first broadcast in 2017.

Church of St Peter and St Paul, Northleach.

3. Clapton-on-the-Hill

Although only a couple of miles south of Bourton-on-the-Water, and fairly near the busy Fosse Way, the tiny village of Clapton-on-the-Hill is little visited by tourists and day trippers. Standing on a hill overlooking the valley of the River Windrush, and with sweeping views from a small green on a steep slope in its centre, it is a particularly peaceful and appealing place.

The largest house in the village is Manor Farm, an admirable dwelling of the seventeenth century. There are a couple more fine farmhouses, as well as some large eighteenth-century barns of local stone. The twelfth-century Church of St James, with its stone roof and stone-clad turret, is among the smallest in Gloucestershire and, with a nave measuring a mere 30 feet by 13, seats only forty-five people. The south doorway, with its lintel and small tympanum, is twelfth century.

The most unusual feature of the church is a thirteenth-century Latin inscription carved onto the northern part of the chancel arch. It says that anyone who, three times and on his knees, devoutly says Father and Hail, will receive a reward then and there of a thousand days. Quite an incentive for regular prayer! There is the base of a medieval cross in the churchyard, which, as if to emphasise its rural location, is entered through a gate made of horseshoes.

Pleasant walks can be taken across the fields to Bourton-on-the-Water and, a little to the south-east of the village, a quiet lane leads downhill to Great Rissington, 2 miles to the east. Marked as 'unsuitable for motors', the lane crosses the River Windrush at New Bridge, which dates to 1840. Serene and unspoilt, the bridge is in a timeless location, with its views of the gently flowing river offering ample reward for the drive along a somewhat unserviceable roadway.

Church of
St James,
Clapton-on-
the-Hill.

Above: View from the village green, Clapton-on-the-Hill.

Below: The River Windrush from New Bridge, Clapton-on-the-Hill.

4. Bourton-on-the-Water

Bourton-on-the-Water is probably the best-known village in the Cotswolds and, as such, receives a steady stream of visitors from America, the Far East and elsewhere in the World – to say nothing of the crowds of British day trippers who regularly descend on the place! All this is hardly surprising, of course, as Bourton is the very epitome of a chocolate-box village. The River Windrush, its banks shaded by leafy trees, contributes much to the scene, as it unhurriedly flows past cottages of honey-coloured stone and beneath elegant low-arched bridges. Anyone wishing to see Bourton at its quietest, though, might like to consider visiting outside the peak holiday season.

An area called Salmonsbury, to the east of the present-day village centre, was a fortified camp in the Iron Age and, during the Roman occupation, Bourton became the site of a Romano-British settlement. The area around Bourton Bridge and the adjacent Fosse Way was densely occupied, where the Romans created a paved ford, footbridge and posting station. Later, during the medieval period, Bourton's economy was almost entirely agricultural until, with the opening of a railway station in 1881, the tourist industry became increasingly significant.

Bourton has a number of visitor attractions, including – behind the Old New Inn – the famous model village, built to one-ninth scale and opened in 1937.

The River Windrush at Bourton-on-the-Water.

Lake beside Greystones Farm nature reserve, Bourton-on-the-Water.

Additionally, there is the Cotswold Motoring Museum at the Old Mill in Sherborne Street, which is home to the miniature car *Brum*, while, sited in Rissington Road, Birdland Park and Gardens first opened in 1957 and is home to over 500 birds, including flamingos, pelicans and penguins. For many discerning visitors, however, the real gem among the village attractions will be Greystones Farm Nature Reserve, owned by Gloucestershire Wildlife Trust and found at the end of Greystones Lane. Situated on the site of Salmonsbury Camp mentioned above, it is home to wildflower meadows (with rare orchids in June), Iron Age ramparts, a replica Iron Age roundhouse, a working organic farm, an interactive Discovery Barn and a courtyard café. The little River Eye flows gently through the reserve, with a nearby lake – much-populated by wildfowl – completing the idyllic scene. (Further information is available online at www.gloucestershirewildlifetrust.co.uk/greystones.)

5. The Slaughters

The lovely, much-photographed village of Lower Slaughter is situated 1.5 miles to the north of Bourton-on-the-Water. Slightly larger, Upper Slaughter village is around a mile north-west, the River Eye being a prominent feature in both of the Slaughter villages. At Upper Slaughter there is a shallow and photogenic ford, with a very small footbridge adjacent, while at Lower Slaughter the river is famously crossed by several simple bridges that link the two sides of the village.

Above: The Mill and River Eye at Lower Slaughter.

Below: The Ford at Upper Slaughter.

Lower Slaughter's Church of St Mary is not of great antiquity, having been rebuilt in the nineteenth century. The nearby Manor House (now a hotel), however, is a grand, symmetrical house of the seventeenth century. Many of the village cottages are from the seventeenth century and are found on the north bank of the river, around a small green called The Square. The green featured prominently in the movie *Tawny Pipit* (1944), and even now, three-quarters of a century later, has changed very little. At the upper end of the village, close to where the road begins climbing Becky Hill, an early nineteenth-century red-brick corn mill, with a still-working metal waterwheel, stands beside the river. This quintessential Cotswold village scene has appeared in many a book on the area.

Upper Slaughter is less busy with visitors than its neighbour, but is equally lovely. The fourteenth-century Church of St Peter was restored in the 1870s, but retains many original features. The village has several notable large houses, including the early seventeenth-century Upper Slaughter Manor and the early eighteenth-century Lords of the Manor Hotel, while at Bagshot's Square a group of eight cottages were remodelled in 1906–13 by distinguished architect Sir Edward Lutyens. Upper Slaughter was used as a location in the movies *Joseph Andrews* (1977) and *The Sailor's Return* (1978).

Many may wonder at the origin of the Slaughter name, assuming it to be associated with some dreadful massacre. The reality is rather more prosaic. It is believed to derive from the Old English word '*slothre*', meaning 'wet land' or 'muddy place'. The diminutive River Eye – probably the cause of the muddiness – meanwhile continues its journey to join the River Dikler to the east of Bourton-on-the-Water.

6. The Guitings (Guiting Power and Temple Guiting)

Situated around 13 miles east of Cheltenham, the unspoilt villages of Guiting Power and Temple Guiting stand around 3 miles apart on the road between Naunton and Winchcombe. 'Guiting', in old English, means 'a flooded place', while 'Power' comes from the Norman 'le Poer' lord of the manor in the early thirteenth century.

Guiting Power, the larger of the two settlements, stands on sloping ground above a valley formed by a tributary of the River Windrush, and is centred mainly on a small green and square. The original Saxon settlement was situated a little to the south-east, close to the late Norman Church of St Michael and All Angels. An archaeological examination in 1990 at a meadow close to the church revealed a small eleventh-century chapel consisting of a rectangular nave and a semi-circular apse – from which the priest would have addressed the worshippers. Clearly visible nearby is a circular mound and ditch representing a defensive ringwork of a similar date. The outline of the Saxon chapel is delineated by reconstructed stone walls.

Both villages are well catered-for in terms of amenities. Guiting Power has a bakery, post office and café, and pub, while Temple Guiting – which takes its name from when, in the twelfth century, a monastic house of the Knights Templar was founded here – has a very good shop and tearoom called The Pantry, a real hidden gem where one can obtain fine food and beverages in a peaceful rural setting. The River Windrush flows along a wooded valley through the centre of the village, being shaded by beech trees and crossed by a road bridge. Near this bridge the river has, at some point in history, been substantially widened to provide a fishing lake, apparently, for a one-time owner of the manor.

Finally, the Cotswold Farm Park, at Bemborough Farm, to the north-east of Guiting Power, is likely to interest families with children. Run by farmer and television presenter Adam Henson, it was opened by his father, Joe, in 1971 to help protect rare breeds of farm animal. Further information can be obtained online at www.cotswoldfarmpark.co.uk.

The Old Post Office and Tea Rooms, Guiting Power.

7. Stow-on-the-Wold and Maugersbury

Situated on a hilltop 700 feet above sea level, Stow-on-the-Wold is, according to local doggerel, a place 'where the wind blows cold'. Anyone who has visited the place outside the summer season can doubtless vouch for the rhyme's veracity! It is, however, a very pleasant town, centred on the Market Square – around which there are a number of lovely seventeenth- and eighteenth-century buildings. Dating in part to the twelfth century, the Church of St Edward has a sturdy fifteenth-century tower that is visible for miles around the town. A large Crucifixion painting in the south aisle is dated 1610. The building was used to imprison Royalist soldiers overnight following a bloody Civil War battle in and around the town in 1646.

Buildings at The Square, Stow-on-the-Wold.

Half Moon House,
Maugersbury.

Although separate from the town, the hamlet of Maugersbury is only half a mile to the south-east. Developed as a 'model village' around 1800 by Edmund John Chamberlayne, lord of the manor, it is actually an older settlement than Stow-on-the-Wold, and although no evidence of a church has been found, it has a manor house, several cottages, houses and seventeenth-century farmhouses, as well as a striking semicircular building called Half Moon House. Built by Chamberlayne in 1800 as an act of philanthropy, it was originally known as The Crescent and formed a row of four workers' cottages that included a Sunday school room, communal bread oven, furnace and coal store.

A little-used lane, from which there are views south towards Icomb Hill, leads to Stow Hill and the Fosse Way (although this lane is in poor condition and there is a barrier preventing vehicular access to the main road beyond). At its western end, the lane passes above a much overgrown stone arch that is a remnant of a tunnel and walkway, which in the early nineteenth century led to a pleasure garden called The Retreat. This was near the top of the hill, while the ancient St Edward's Well – its waters reputedly beneficial to the eyes – stands in woods near the bottom. It once had a stone gazebo nearby, which, together with the pleasure garden, represented part of Stow's nineteenth-century endeavours to popularise itself as a resort. Today, though, the entire woodland area is heavily overgrown and almost impenetrable. A tree-lined path can be followed, however, from the centre of the hamlet, past Maugersbury Manor, and through a park to Stow's Lower Park Street.

8. Sezincote

An Indian palace-style building, complete with weathered-copper onion dome, is probably not the kind of edifice one expects to see in the Cotswold Hills of Gloucestershire. Sezincote House, just under 3 miles south-west of Moreton-in-Marsh, appears, however, to be just such a place. Visible from quite some distance around, the roof dome – a symbol of peace and tranquility – is characteristic of

Muslim architecture and illustrates the Persian influence. Originally burnished copper, it now has a blue-green patina of verdigris as a result of atmospheric oxidisation.

The house was the brainchild of British nabob Colonel John Cockerell, who returned to England from India in 1795 and bought the Sezincote estate, having amassed a fortune in the East India Company. He died a few years after his return, and the estate passed to his youngest brother, Charles, who had also worked for the company. He commissioned his brother, Samuel, a successful architect, to remodel the existing manor house into an Indian house in the Moghul style of Rajasthan. Samuel worked closely with his artist friend Thomas Daniell, who had spent years in India, making watercolours and oil paintings of Indian buildings and landscapes. These two men drew influence from the sixteenth-century Moghul Emperor Akbar, who had mixed Islamic and Hindu styles in an effort to integrate the cultures.

The resulting building, though planned like an English villa, exhibits many details of Indian Islamic architecture and is quite extraordinary. It is built with beautiful golden-orange stone, quarried from Barrington and, it is said, artificially stained to create an appropriately-Indian tone. Among its features are minarets, peacock-tail windows, jali-work railings and pavilions. The interior of the house, however, is neoclassical Greek. Although a breathtaking representation of Cockerell's great affluence, the grand house displays, too, the man's love and respect of India's architecture and culture.

Sezincote House.

Indian temple and pool at Sezincote House gardens.

The house is set in a magical landscape, and has an Indian sunken water garden designed with assistance from the great landscape artist Humphrey Repton. Among grottoes, waterfalls and canals, there is a pool and fountain near a temple containing a statue of Souriya, the Hindu goddess, and there is a bridge decorated with Brahmin sacred bulls. The garden is alive with a display of bamboos, maples, cedars and a host of exotic plants. The garden became neglected in the Second World War, but was restored in 1968 by Sir Cyril and Lady Kleinwort. It was Lady Kleinwort who, with assistance from Graham Stuart Thomas, created the charming 'Paradise Garden', with its conifer-bordered canal, at the south of the house. Following a visit by the Prince Regent in 1807, Sezincote House became a benchmark for Brighton Pavilion. Fortunately, the house and garden are open to visitors. Further information is available online at www.sezincote.co.uk.

9. Batsford

A small and compact estate village situated on a hill a mile and a half north-west of Moreton-in-Marsh, Batsford consists of Victorian Tudor estate housing clustered around the neo-Norman Church of St Mary. Built in 1860–62 of dressed stone, the church has a tower and spire and stands on a bank near the entrance to the driveway of Batsford Park mansion. Inside the building there is a fine wall monument to Thomas Edward Freeman by sculptor Joseph Nollekens, as well as monuments to members of the Mitford family, the Lords Redesdale, ancestors of the renowned Mitford sisters.

An especially alluring approach to the village, leading off the lane from Moreton-in-Marsh, passes along an avenue of lime trees. Visible across pasture to the west is Batsford Stud, formerly the stables to Batsford Park, built in 1878 by Sir Ernest George. A curved gable, surmounted by a wooden turret over the arched entrance to the courtyard, is a particularly imposing feature of this elegant building.

Although Batsford Park is situated nearby, public access to the arboretum and its amenities is available only through an entrance and driveway off the A44 road between Moreton-in-Marsh and Bourton-on-the-Hill. The Elizabethan-styled mansion – which is not open to the public – was designed by Sir Ernest George and Harold Peto, and was built in 1887–93 for A. B. Freeman-Mitford (later Lord Redesdale), who had been a diplomat in the Far East. It was he who began planting the arboretum and Japanese Gardens in the 1890s.

Sitting on the edge of an escarpment overlooking Batsford Park mansion and the Evenlode Vale beyond, Lord Redesdale's gardens cover some 50 acres and comprise a very large collection of bamboos, shrubs and colourful trees from around the world. Adding to the Far East theme, a Japanese rest house – together with imported bronze statues of Buddha, a Foo Dog and a pair of Japanese sika deer – can be seen on the slope above the mansion. Nearby, sculpted by Simon Verity, is a statue of the nymph goddess Daphne. According to Greek legend, she was turned into a laurel tree when fleeing from the lovestruck Apollo.

Also likely to be of interest to visitors and sited near the arboretum are a Garden Terrace Café, a well-stocked plant centre and the Cotswold Falconry Centre, which has 130 birds of sixty different species and provides regular flying displays. Further information about the arboretum is available online at www.batsarb.co.uk.

Batsford Arboretum.

Above: Chinese Foo Dog at Batsford Arboretum.

Below: The Lime Avenue at Batsford.

10. Chipping Campden

Among the many beautiful towns and villages in the Cotswolds, Chipping Campden must surely rank as one of the loveliest. Its gently curving High Street is lined with beautiful seventeenth- and eighteenth-century houses, the fine Market Hall – built by lord of the manor Sir Baptist Hicks in 1627 – being a particularly pleasing feature. The export of wool was an important local industry in the fourteenth and fifteenth centuries, the town's wealthy wool merchants helping to fund the transformation of the Church of St James into the exceptional building seen today. Much has been written about the church and the fine houses along the High Street, and since almost every building in the town could be considered a gem, the intention here is to highlight a couple of the less obvious features worthy of note.

A series of undulations in uneven ground immediately south of the churchyard – in an area called the Coneygree – mark the remains of what was, until retreating Royalists burnt it to the ground in 1645, one of Chipping Campden's most outstanding buildings. Campden House was an extravagant mansion, with many windows and turrets, built in 1612 for Sir Baptist Hicks. The gateway and lodges

The Market Hall, Chipping Campden.

next to the churchyard survive, however, as well as two banqueting houses. The remaining earthworks indicate the layout of the mansion's grand gardens, which included ornamental canals and a small lake. A causeway led to Lady Juliana's Gateway, which survives and stands isolated in a field. Poignantly atmospheric, this is one of Chipping Campden's most enchanting features.

A discreet and unusual little public garden can be visited at an area called Leysbourne, at the north end of the High Street. Once part of the vicarage grounds, the Ernest Wilson Memorial Garden was opened in 1984 to commemorate notable botanist Ernest Henry 'Chinese' Wilson, who was born at Chipping Campden in 1876. He subsequently moved to Birmingham, where he began his career at the Botanical Gardens, going on to travel to China and the Far East in search of unusual plants. He went on to become keeper of the Arnold Arboretum at the USA's Harvard University, but never returned to Chipping Campden and was tragically killed with his wife in a car crash in 1930. Although less than an acre in size, the Memorial Garden has many plants that were discovered or introduced by Wilson, ensuring there is always something of interest to be seen.

Entrance to Ernest Wilson Memorial Garden, Chipping Campden.

Lady Juliana's Gate, Chipping Campden.

11. Hidcote Bartrim

The tiny village of Hidcote Bartrim is situated at the northern edge of the Cotswold escarpment, some 3 miles north-east of Chipping Campden, and has excellent views over the Vale of Evesham. These can be seen from a lane-side viewpoint that looks down to a wooded valley called Weeping Hollow and on towards Mickleton village at the foot of the slope. Weeping Hollow is, according to many folklore accounts, the haunt of a ghost known as the Mickleton Hooter, which has often been heard screeching and howling. Weeping Hollow may indeed be home to some hellish supernatural entity, but many may prefer to believe the more rational explanation that natural sounds are sometimes amplified by the funnel effect of the steep-sided valley.

Most visitors to Hidcote Bartrim, however, come to see its two famous gardens. The slightly better known of the two is the National Trust's Hidcote Manor Garden – actually a series of small gardens separated by mellow walls and clipped hedges – created by the great horticulturist Major Lawrence Johnston following his mother's purchase of the seventeenth-century house in 1907. Although Johnston initially had no special horticultural expertise, he worked earnestly on the project, which reached fruition in the early 1920s. The result was a series of outdoor 'rooms' that included, among others, the Fuchsia Garden, the Bathing Pool Garden, the Red Borders, Mrs Winthrop's Garden and the Pillar Garden. Lawns, mature trees, brilliant flower beds, gazebos and wrought-iron gates combine to render Hidcote Manor Garden truly memorable. (Further information is available online at www.natonaltrust.org.uk/hidcote.)

Hidcote's second notable garden – created by three generations of women gardeners – is at nearby Kiftsgate Court. Sitting on the very edge of the escarpment above Mickleton, the mainly Victorian house has two bold eighteenth-century wings that were transported piece by piece from Mickleton Manor, far below, on a specially constructed light railway. Each wing features a projecting portico supported by a row of columns reminiscent of Greek architecture. Steps lead down to beautiful gardens on two different levels – the lower garden enjoying spectacular views over the vale below. The dramatic hillside setting of the gardens does, however, render some especially steep, uneven and slippery areas inaccessible to people with mobility difficulties. (Further information is available online at www.kiftsgate.co.uk.)

Weeping Hollow from Hidcote Bartrim.

Above: Hidcote Manor Gardens.

Below: The Great Lawn at Hidcote Manor Gardens.

12. Snowshill

A lovely hillside village of pretty cottages and houses gathered around the churchyard and village green, Snowshill is situated 5 miles south-west of Chipping Campden and only around 2 miles south of Broadway, in neighbouring Worcestershire. To some it may be recognised as a location used in the movie *Bridget Jones's Diary* (2001), but it is probable that many visitors come primarily to see the National Trust's popular property Snowshill Manor. This curious and somewhat odd-looking house, which dates to around 1500, was a possession of Winchcombe Abbey until the Dissolution of the Monasteries in 1539. The house has long been the subject of folklore accounts, with Ann's Room said to have been the setting of an illegal marriage ceremony in 1604 – the bride's ghost supposedly haunting the place ever since.

In 1919 the house – in semi-derelict condition – was purchased by eccentric collector Charles Wade, who used it to accommodate his huge and ever-growing collection of antiques, toys, samurai armour, timepieces, unusual artefacts and curiosities. It seems that Wade was something of a 'human magpie', who seized upon almost anything that caught his interest. It has been said, too, that he had an interest in alchemy, astrology and magic – such rumours helping reinforce the manor's reputation as a place of mystery. Certainly an attic room known as The Witch's Garrett – not usually open to the public – exists at the top of the house, where a wall is decorated with mystic symbols. An obscure circular design connected with Rosicrucianism is painted on the floor, and various items of necromantic paraphernalia are displayed nearby.

Wade was an advocate of the Arts and Crafts movement, so he employed these influences when restoring the house. Further, he commissioned the Arts and Crafts architect M. H. Baillie-Scott to transform the garden wilderness into a series of terraces and interconnecting 'rooms' with flower beds and climbing plants. Wade presented the house and its contents to the National Trust in 1951. He died in 1956 and is buried in the graveyard of Snowshill Church. (Further information is available online at www.nationaltrust.org.uk/snowshill-manor-and-garden.)

Snowshill Village.

13. Stanway

Stanway Hill is a winding, tree-lined slope that runs down the escarpment from the Cotswold Hills towards Tewkesbury and the Severn Vale. From the top there are fine views towards Winchcombe and the Malvern Hills beyond, while, near the foot of the hill, the small and quiet village of Stanway is found near a crossroads. Prominently standing on a green next to the crossroads is an elegant war memorial of 1920. It consists of an outstanding bronze sculpture of St George and the Dragon by Alexander Fisher, surmounted on a stone column and plinth by Sir Philip Stott, with finely crafted lettering by Eric Gill. This really is a most striking monument.

Nearby, Stanway House is an interesting Jacobean manor house that was built between the late sixteenth century and mid-seventeenth century. Its imposing gatehouse, immediately visible as one descends the road from the war memorial, is a remarkable building of three storeys, with three shaped gables and a central archway. It was probably built between 1630 and1640 and is believed to be the work of Timothy Strong of Taynton. Within the grounds of the house are a fourteenth-century tithe barn, an eighteenth-century water garden and a spectacular single-jet fountain that, at 300 feet, is the highest fountain in the UK and the highest gravity fountain in the world. The house is regularly opened to the public (see notice at the entrance or check online at www.stanwayfountain.co.uk).

The gatehouse at Stanway House.

The war memorial at Stanway.

A completely different kind of gem can be seen around half a mile to the west and just off the B4077 road. Toddington railway station, built in 1904, was formerly on the Great Western Railway's Honeybourne Line, which operated from 1906 to 1976 between Cheltenham, Stratford-upon-Avon and Birmingham. The volunteer-run Gloucestershire-Warwickshire Railway was formed soon after the line's 1976 closure and in 1984 started steam train operations over a short distance. By 2018 the heritage line ran between Cheltenham Racecourse, Winchcombe and Broadway, running regular train services every weekend. A variety of steam and heritage diesel locomotives are operated, including, on past occasions, the world-famous locomotives *Flying Scotsman* and *City of Truro*. (For further information check www.gwsr.com.)

14. The Sudeley Valley

A popular walking route and one of the hidden gems of the North Cotswolds, the beautiful Sudeley Valley runs for around 2.5 miles between Winchcombe on its northern edge and the villages of Charlton Abbots and Brockhampton to the south. The narrow and relatively little-used Corndean Lane follows a pretty route along the valley's western slopes, providing good views towards Sudeley Castle and the unspoilt rural landscape beyond. High above on the eastern edge, meanwhile, a quiet road runs from Roel Gate and down Sudeley Hill to Winchcombe. From this road there are panoramic views over the valley towards Cleeve Common and to the Malvern Hills. When stopping to admire the scene, the only sounds generally heard are the calls of larks and buzzards in the skies overhead.

Winchcombe was a place of great importance in Saxon times, being the capital of Winchcombshire in the Kingdom of Mercia for a brief period in the eleventh century. A great abbey was founded in the town around AD 798, but this was demolished after the Dissolution of the Monasteries and nothing now remains. The Church of St Peter was rebuilt around 1460–70 and has an imposing west tower that is some 90 feet high. There are a number of interesting features within the building, including two stone coffins found on the abbey site in 1815 and said to have contained the bodies of the Mercian King Kenulf and his son St Kenelm. At the west end of the nave there is an ornately carved medieval oak screen, and a former altar cloth stitched by Catherine of Aragon can be seen in a cabinet near the north door. Outside, the many grotesques and gargoyles embellishing the battlemented roofline form a particularly unusual and amusing collection.

At the south of the town the fifteenth-century Sudeley Castle, standing on the site of an earlier fortification, is open to the public. Most famously it was the home of Henry VIII's widow Katherine Parr, when in 1547 she married its occupant, Thomas Seymour. She died in 1548 and her restored tomb, which was desecrated in the Civil War, can be seen in St Mary's Chapel. The castle became ruinous after being damaged by the Parliamentarians, but was later restored when two Worcester brothers, John and William Dent, bought the estate in 1837. (Further information is available online at www.sudeleycastle.co.uk.)

The Sudeley Valley has several sites of historical interest. Footpaths off Corndean Lane lead to the well-preserved Neolithic chambered long barrow at Belas Knap and the remains of Roman villas at Wadfield and Spoonley Wood. These monuments are not easy to access, however, so many may prefer to take a leisurely drive along this lovely route, culminating, perhaps, in a visit to Brockhampton's well-regarded Craven Arms pub.

Winchcombe and the Malvern Hills seen from the Sudeley Valley's eastern edge.

Above: Sudeley Castle seen from Corndean Lane.

Below: Grotesque at the Church of St Peter, Winchcombe.

South Cotswolds

15. Crickley Hill and Barrow Wake

Two of Gloucestershire's fine viewpoints are situated within a fairly short distance of each other on high ground some 4 miles south of Cheltenham. Both locations – which jointly form a 140-acre biological and geological Site of Special Scientific Interest (SSSI) – provide panoramic views over Gloucester, the Severn Vale and beyond to the Welsh Mountains and Malvern Hills. They are managed in partnership by the Gloucestershire Wildlife Trust and the National Trust.

The first viewpoint is at Crickley Hill Country Park, off the B4070 Leckhampton Hill road from Cheltenham and near the notoriously busy Air Balloon roundabout. The site is on a prominent spur of the Cotswold escarpment, its rocky exposures forming part of a key Jurassic locality. An elevated viewpoint, easily accessible from the car parking area, provides an excellent outlook. Public facilities include a picnic area, with a café and lavatories in a small building nearby.

From a biological perspective, it is one of the finest unimproved limestone grassland areas in the county, with several species of orchid having been recorded here. Crickley Hill supports a rich diversity of wild flowers and has a good population of butterflies, adders and slow worms. Circular walks can be taken through the various areas of grassland and woodland. Additionally, Crickley Hill is the site of an Iron Age fortified village that had been constructed by 2500 BC. This is an important archaeological site that has been studied in detail. Precisely when the village came to an end is uncertain, but it was undoubtedly violent. Archaeologists have found many arrowheads, as well as evidence that the place was razed by fire. (Further information is available online at www.nationaltrust.org.uk/crickley-hill.)

The second viewpoint site, with abundant flora and sweeping views over the Severn Vale, is less than a mile south-west on the A417 road to Cirencester. Known as Barrow Wake, it has ample car parking facilities, as well as a stone indicator that illustrates the area's geology. The dramatic rock face of Crickley Hill can be seen to the north-west. It was at a quarry near Barrow Wake viewpoint that the famous bronze Birdlip Mirror (dated around AD 50) was found by workmen in 1879. Considered one of the finest examples of Celtic art to survive in Britain, it can be seen in Gloucester City Museum. (Further information is available online at www.gloucestershirewildlifetrust.co.uk/nature-reserves/barrow-wake.)

Above: Viewpoint at Crickley Hill Country Park.

Below: Crickley Hill and Iron Age fort seen from Barrow Wake.

16. Bisley

A picturesque hillside village on the north side of the valley of the River Frome, some 4 miles to the east of Stroud, Bisley enjoyed prosperity through the seventeenth and eighteenth centuries when the local cloth-weaving cottage industry was at its height. This declined rapidly, however, when cloth mills embraced mechanisation with the advent of power looms, and mass unemployment led to considerable local poverty. It is likely that this led to a rise in petty crime, with wrongdoers being dealt with at the manor court, which met at the Bear Inn, George Street, from 1766 to 1838. Conveniently near the inn, which has a pleasing façade consisting of an overhanging portico supported by seventeenth-century columns, is the village lock-up. Dated 1824, with an ogee gable and ball-finial, it has two cells – one for men, the other for women – for people awaiting trial before the magistrates. It is rare that a place of imprisonment can be termed a gem, but this appealing little building surely deserves the honour.

Bisley is full of attractive stone dwellings, with many of the houses in the narrow High Street dating to the seventeenth or early eighteenth century. Most of the thirteenth-century Church of All Saints was reconstructed in the 1860s, but it retains a number of interesting features. It may indeed stand on the site of a Roman temple. Two Roman altars – now in the British Museum – were excavated near the tower in the nineteenth century, and some carved Saxon stones are displayed in the south aisle. At the bottom of the bowl of the elaborately carved Norman font are two fish carved in relief, while standing outside in the churchyard is a curious thirteenth-century structure known as the poor souls' light, in which candles for the dead were once placed.

Bisley Wells, at the roadside just below the church, date to 1863 and are made up of seven fountain heads in a row. An ancient well dressing ceremony takes place each Ascension Day, when a procession of children bearing garlands of flowers gather at the wells for a service of blessing. A rarity in Gloucestershire, this custom is much more common in the Peak District of Derbyshire and Staffordshire.

The village lock-up, Bisley.

Bisley Wells
decorated with
flowers after the
Ascension Day
well-dressing
ceremony.

17. Painswick

The small town of Painswick, 3 miles north of Stroud, sits on the side of a spur overlooking the Painswick Stream, and has beautiful views over the valley. Reflecting its former prosperity as a medieval wool town and later the centre of a thriving cloth industry, its narrow streets are lined with lovely seventeenth- and eighteenth-century houses, built of the local grey-white stone from a quarry on Painswick Beacon. When the cloth industry declined in the mid-nineteenth century, however, Painswick became popular as a residential area for the well-heeled retired and professional classes working in Gloucester, Cheltenham and Stroud.

The fifteenth-century Church of St Mary, with its soaring spire, is particularly interesting. The original spire was erected in 1632, but had to be rebuilt twice following lightning strikes in 1763 and 1883. The church building saw Civil War action in 1644 when Royalist troops besieged it, using cannon and firebombs to drive out the Parliamentarians quartered inside. Impressions left by cannon balls can still be seen below the clock face on the tower.

The churchyard's colonnade of ninety-nine clipped yew trees, mostly planted around 1792, is very well known in Gloucestershire. Each Sunday following 19 September the traditional Clypping ceremony takes place in the churchyard, in which children with garlands, together with the clergy and choir, sing traditional hymns and hold hands to encircle the church – 'Clyppan' is an Anglo-Saxon term meaning 'to encircle' or 'embrace'. This custom has been performed intermittently since the early nineteenth century. Also of note in the churchyard is an unsurpassed collection of table and pedestal tombs, mostly from the late seventeenth century or eighteenth century. Near the Court House in Hale Lane, close to the churchyard, is a rare set of iron spectacle stocks dating to the seventeenth century.

Painswick Beacon to the north of the town consists of 250 acres of common land, with views over the Severn Vale and beyond to the Welsh mountains. An extensive Iron Age hill fort, which has clearly discernible banks and ditches, occupies the summit of the beacon. A car park nearby can be accessed from the B4073 road. Also accessible from this road is the quirky and fascinating eighteenth-century Rococo Garden at Painswick House, dating to the early eighteenth century. (Further information is available online at www.rococogarden.org.uk.)

Left: New Street, Painswick.

Below: Tombs and clipped yews at Painswick churchyard.

18. Woodchester

Standing on the west side of the Nailsworth Valley 2 miles south of Stroud, the village of Woodchester is chiefly known for its superb Roman mosaic pavement. Depicting Orpheus playing his lyre, it was discovered in the late eighteenth century among the remains of a palatial villa lying beneath the old Church of St Mary. This Norman church was abandoned in 1863 and subsequently demolished, leaving only the few evocative ruins visible today. For its preservation, the mosaic lies buried under the soil of the churchyard. It used to be uncovered periodically for public viewing, but this no longer takes place. Most of the finds from the villa are in the British Museum.

Comparably well known is the unfinished mansion at Woodchester Park. Situated in a remote valley, this hauntingly atmospheric Victorian Gothic house stands exactly as it was when, around 1870, work on the building came to an abrupt halt. As if in some kind of eerie time warp, abandoned ladders still stand propped against interior walls. What, one may ask, caused this sudden stoppage?

In 1845 William Leigh, the wealthy owner of the estate, had commissioned local architect Benjamin Bucknall to build the mansion in the style of French architect Eugene Viollet-le-Duc. By 1858 work was three-quarters complete, but it seems that funds ran low. Additionally, Leigh was in poor health and doctors advised him against living in the damp valley. He died in 1873 and his son, who inherited the house, decided against spending money on its completion. It remained empty, lifeless and deteriorating for more than a century until, in 1987, it was bought by Stroud District Council to save it from ruin and was subsequently acquired by the Woodchester Mansion Trust. Open to the public, it is a fascinating – if spookily lifeless – property in a beautiful location.

Almost inevitably, numerous ghost stories and accounts of paranormal activity have been reported and there have been several investigations by interested societies and organisations. Although results have not always been convincing, some recorded events have suggested there may be more to Woodchester Park than first meets the eye. (Further information is available online at www.woodchestermansion.org.uk.)

The unfinished mansion at Woodchester Park.

19. Uley

The valley in which Uley nestles was a centre of industrial activity in the seventeenth and eighteenth centuries, and numerous cloth mills were situated on the River Ewelme. In 1608 twenty-nine Uley weavers were producing cloth to be marketed by local clothiers – their blue broadcloth being especially prized – and at a peak in the early nineteenth century a mill run by one Edward Sheppard had a workforce of almost 1,000 people. Its financial collapse in 1837, however, led to rapid industrial decline and none of the cloth mills have survived.

Uley's eleventh-century stone church was demolished and replaced with the present Church of St Giles in 1857–58. Perched on the slope above the valley, it is one of the nicer looking Victorian churches in Gloucestershire, with a bold tower, fine nave roof, some good stained-glass windows and an octagonal font bowl of around 1200. There are some fine chest tombs in the churchyard. Little more than a stone's throw from the church is a small green, beside which there are several pleasing eighteenth-century houses, as well as a seventeenth-century traditional inn called the Old Crown.

A substantial Iron Age hill fort known as Uley Bury is situated on a spur of the escarpment above the village. One of the largest Iron Age forts in Gloucestershire, it stands some 800 feet above sea level and has a double line of 4-foot-high earth

Village green and Old Crown Inn, Uley.

Tomb entrance at Hetty Pegler's Tump.

ramparts and ditches that enclose an area of 38 acres. The fort has never been fully excavated, although a gold coin and some pottery sherds of Iron Age date have been found in the interior area. Panoramic views over the Severn Vale can be seen from the ramparts – and from nearby Coaley Wood – which can be reached by following a path off a lay-by next to the B4066 road.

A Neolithic chambered long barrow called Hetty Pegler's Tump can be seen around a mile to the north of the church. At least 5,000 years old, the barrow is 120 feet long and has a central passageway leading to an end chamber and two side chambers. Although the monument is visually impressive and is one of a small number of long barrow tombs that one can actually enter, it has suffered vandalism and inexpert excavation over a great many years. Even so, it remains a fascinating example of a chambered barrow. Between fifteen and twenty skeletons have been discovered in the tomb, but the bones are thought to have been reburied in Uley churchyard. It takes its name from a seventeenth-century landowner named Hester Pegler, who owned the ground on which it stands.

20. Owlpen

Just half a mile to the east of Uley, the beautifully remote village of Owlpen is found in a deep hollow, surrounded on three sides by woodland. It is approached by narrow grass-grown lanes, leading one to imagine the epithets secret village and hidden gem were coined with Owlpen in mind. In addition to its timeless setting, this tiny settlement is notable for its enchanting manor house and richly decorated Victorian church.

One of Gloucestershire's most picturesque manor houses, Owlpen Manor dates to the fifteenth century, during which period the lords of the manor were the de Olepenne family. Heiress Margery Olepenne – the last of the medieval Olepennes – was married to John Daunt, of a Wotton-under-Edge merchant family, sometime after 1464 and it was possibly this that occasioned the building of the house.

The Daunts were actually much wealthier than the Olepennes. A later Daunt remodelled the house in 1616, with further remodelling occurring in 1719. It was mainly uninhabited in the nineteenth century and became increasingly derelict over an eighty-year period, but in 1925 was saved from ruin when it was bought by architect Norman Jewson. Helped by local craftsmen, he restored it in the Arts and Crafts style, and it was subsequently sold on.

Queen Margaret, wife of Henry VI, is said to have stayed at the house with her son, Prince Edward, in 1471. Perhaps unsurprisingly, there are various ghost stories connected with the place. Today Owlpen Manor – along with its eighteenth-century terraced gardens and clipped yew trees – is carefully preserved by its owners, Sir Nicholas and Lady Mander, and their son, Hugo, who runs the estate. In 2017 the house was used as a filming location for the period drama movie *Phantom Thread*, starring Daniel Day-Lewis. Although Owlpen Manor is not generally open to the public, group visits to the house can be arranged if pre-booked. Its garden, however, is routinely open to visitors on weekday afternoons. (Further information is available online at www.owlpen.com.)

The Victorian Church of the Holy Cross stands on a bank just above the manor house. It has a particularly rich interior, the ceiling of the chancel being painted with star patterns and sunbursts, and its walls enriched with inlaid mosaics. The walls of the baptistery are lined with even more elaborate mosaics, while an alabaster cross on the altar is ornamented with twenty-nine amethysts. The headstone of a grave in the churchyard is decorated with a bronze bee, designed by Bryant Fedden. In various faiths and religions bees are thought to symbolise attributes such as love and harmony.

Owlpen Manor and Church of the Holy Cross.

21. Nailsworth

A fairly small town 3.5 miles south of Stroud, Nailsworth was busy in the eighteenth century with a number of productive cloth mills in operation, although these have long since closed and other uses have been found for the buildings. The town centre remains busy, however, and has various interesting and individual shops. A tall clock tower on the green in the town centre was erected in 1951 in memory of those who fell in the two world wars. Egypt Mill, on the Stroud Road, contains two large iron working waterwheels and has been sympathetically converted to provide accommodation and a welcoming riverside bar and restaurant.

Dunkirk Mill, in the Nailsworth Valley, is a substantial and impressive multi-storey mill building – the earliest part of which dates to 1797. Found by the Stroud Road, almost a mile north-west of the town, the mill buildings have now been sympathetically concerted to apartments. The Dunkirk Mill Centre at the site enables visitors to see a massive working waterwheel that directly powers a rare piece of historic textile machinery. The 12-foot-wide overshot wheel was installed in the mill in 1855 during its time as a woollen mill.

Ruskin Mill, on the Old Bristol Road a little way to the south-west, has a restored waterwheel and overlooks a large mill pool that is much populated by ducks. A popular and well-regarded coffee shop offering tasty and healthy food has a balcony overlooking the pool. For over thirty years the Ruskin Mill Trust has provided specialist independent education to children and adults with complex needs. A real hidden gem of a place, Ruskin Mill – formerly known as Millbottom Mill – is well worth visiting.

Egypt Mill, Nailsworth.

The mill pool seen from the café balcony at Ruskin Mill, Nailsworth.

22. Westonbirt Arboretum

Accessed from the A433 Cirencester to Bath road, 3 miles south-west of Tetbury, The National Arboretum at Westonbirt is at the southernmost tip of Gloucestershire, near the boundary with Wiltshire. One of the best-known arboretums in the UK, its extensive plant collection comprises around 18,000 trees and shrubs spread over its 600-acre area. Two main avenues, Jackson Avenue and Holford Ride, run through the arboretum, which is navigated over 17 miles of marked trails and paths. Great care has been taken to plant the many different-coloured species – such as azaleas, rhododendrons, magnolias and maples – in a well-balanced way, creating an overall effect of harmony.

The arboretum is home to various national tree collections, which consist of groups of trees that the arboretum has undertaken to document, develop and preserve. Among these are maples, walnuts and limes – the Chinese lime, which has unusual peeling bark, is the arboretum's rarest specimen. Regrettably, many trees throughout the world are in danger of extinction. Westonbirt holds around 100 threatened species, allowing researchers to study how they grow, helping to inform decisions on how to best care for them. Two of the rarest of these critically endangered trees are the sapphire dragon tree and the Madeira mountain ash.

Westonbirt Arboretum's sheer size and scale mean it is not possible to see everything in a single visit. Staff and volunteers are on hand, however, with advice and suggestions as to which areas offer the best sights at each season. In springtime, of course, many plants start bursting into life after their winter slumbers, while autumn is spectacular for the magical displays of leaf colour. Westonbirt's size and diversity, however, ensures there is something interesting to see at any time of year – some species of maple, for example, display wonderful bark patterns that look their best in winter.

The arboretum, begun in 1829, was the creation of wealthy landowner Robert Holford of Westonbirt House. After his death, his son, Sir George Holford, and Sir George's nephew, the 4th Earl Morley, oversaw the care and continuing expansion of the arboretum until, in 1956, the Forestry Commission took on the care and management of the vast plant collection for the benefit of the nation. (Further information is available online at www.forestryengland.uk/westonbirt-the-national-arboretum.)

Right: Westonbirt's Old Arboretum.

Below: Acer trees dwarfed by the trunk of an American pine at Westonbirt Arboretum.

23. Coates

The River Thames rises in a meadow known as Trewsbury Mead, at Thames Head in the parish of Coates. Little more than a muddy depression beneath a tree, it is marked by a granite slab that declares the site to be the true source. This location is easily found by following a footpath from near the Thames Head Inn on the A433 Tetbury Road.

Coates village, a little north of the Thames source, is 3 miles west of Cirencester. The Church of St Matthew, on the north-western edge of the village, has a fine Perpendicular tower, complete with battlements and elegant pinnacles, thought to be of the fifteenth century. The Norman south doorway, with its chevron-moulded arch, is believed the oldest part of the building, while the bowl of the font is believed to date to around 1200.

A curious feature at Coates is a section of the Thames and Severn Canal that enters a canal tunnel, which runs for over 2.25 miles through the Cotswold hills before coming out at Sapperton. The canal was opened in 1789 to link the Stroudwater Canal at Stroud with the Thames, near Lechlade, and the canal tunnel was at that time the longest ever constructed in the UK. Made with large stone blocks, the tunnel portal at

Canal tunnel entrance, Coates.

The Tunnel House, Coates.

Coates is quite ornate, with Doric columns and a rusticated archway. The portal was restored by the Cotswold Canals Trust in 1976, although is now somewhat overgrown.

The tunnel is 14 feet 4 inches wide, with a minimum height of 15 feet 4 inches, and, as there is no towpath in the interior, bargees would propel the boats by lying on their backs and pushing with their feet against the tunnel roof – a procedure that took more than three hours to complete. Although the canal tunnel was a significant engineering achievement of its day, its efficiency was hampered by frequent water level problems and the canal was never a great success. The last commercial boats to use the tunnel were in 1911 and by 1916 it was impassable to normal boat traffic. The entire canal was abandoned in 1927 and today the tunnel remains partially blocked following significant roof falls. The interesting Tunnel House Inn, on ground above the portal, was built in the 1770s for the canal navvies and bargees.

24. Cirencester

A busy market town and popular centre for tourism, Cirencester possesses a number of interesting shops and places to eat. There is no shortage of green spaces either, with Abbey Grounds, Cirencester Park and St Michael's Park all within easy reach of the town centre. During the Roman occupation the town was known as Corinium Dobunnorum. Its streets were laid out in the last quarter of the first century AD, and then, towards the end of the second century AD, the town became the capital of one of the provinces into which Britain had been divided. It was, in fact, the second largest city by area in Roman Britain. Surprisingly little evidence of Roman Cirencester survives above ground, although there is a stretch of the Roman town wall on the far side of Abbey Grounds and a turf-covered Roman amphitheatre – which would have accommodated around 8,000 people – can be seen to the west of the town. This is best accessed from Cotswold Avenue. For a real flavour of Roman Cirencester, however, a visit to the superb Corinium Museum in Park Street is recommended.

During the medieval period Cirencester became a prosperous wool town. The cathedral-like Church of St John the Baptist, which dominates the town centre, is Gloucestershire's largest parish church. The earliest church on the site was probably started in the twelfth century, but the existing building dates from the fifteenth and sixteenth centuries. With its imposing tower, rising 162 feet above the market square, and its majestic south porch, it is among the finest of the Cotswold wool churches.

Cirencester Park, the family seat of the Earls of Bathurst, is an early eighteenth-century landscape park, some 3,000 acres in size, and is considered the finest of its kind in England. Its main feature is its Broad Avenue, which stretches from the park gates to the horizon 5 miles distant. A path called Broad Ride, entered from the park's entrance at the top of Cecily Hill, is, however, more manageable at around a mile in length. Although Cirencester Park mansion is not open to the public, the parkland is free for pedestrians to walk in between 8.00 a.m. and 5.00 p.m. Dotted around the park are various interesting monuments and follies, including a rusticated pavilion known as Pope's Seat, and a curious structure with six arched openings, called the Hexagon – both dated to around 1736. Queen Anne's Monument, erected in 1741, is a 50-foot-high Doric column that us crowned with a statue of the queen. A rural gem close to the heart of the town, Cirencester Park is one of its principal attractions.

Abbey Grounds, Cirencester.

Above: Market Place and Church of St John, Cirencester.

Below: Cirencester Park.

25. Bibury

Bibury is another of the Gloucestershire honeypot villages that prove irresistible to the many tourists determined to visit every iconic Cotswold location. This is completely understandable, however, as Bibury has for years been lauded as one of the loveliest villages in the area. Eighteenth-century English poet Alexander Pope spoke of its 'pleasing prospect' and, later, William Morris, the eminent Victorian poet, craftsman and proponent of the Arts and Crafts movement – who liked to walk around Bibury and its surrounds – called it 'surely the most beautiful village in England'.

Situated in the winding valley of the River Coln, 6 miles to the north-east of Cirencester, the village has a number of interesting Cotswold stone buildings. The B4425 road to Cirencester passes through the centre of Bibury, the river flowing alongside on its way to join the Thames near Lechlade. The river, often populated by swans and moorhens, is crossed by a small three-arched stone footbridge that leads to the famous Arlington Row and on up Awkward Hill. The road crosses the river a little further along by a three-arched stone bridge of 1770.

Arlington Row, Bibury.

The quaint and much-photographed Arlington Row dates to the fourteenth century, having originally been built as a wool store. The store's conversion into cottages is thought to have occurred in the sixteenth and seventeenth centuries. Formerly occupied by weavers, the undulating row consists of nine small, irregularly shaped cottages with steep-pitched roofs and gables.

To the front of the cottages is Rack Isle, used at one time for drying cloth on wooden racks after it had been worked by the weavers. Rack Isle is today a boggy water meadow that provides an important habitat for wildlife, such as kingfishers, water voles, dragonflies and grass snakes. A small herd of naturally docile Belted Galloway cattle graze the Rack Isle in late summer. Bibury Trout Farm, nearby, is a popular visitor attraction.

Beautifully secluded on the east side of the village, the Church of St Mary is of much interest. It has Saxon origins and was extensively rebuilt in the twelfth and thirteenth centuries. A survival of the Saxon church can be seen built into a shallow pillar on the north side of the chancel. This is part of a finely sculptured gravestone, decorated with interlacing circles, that was reset here around 1913. Also of interest are the Norman north and south doorways and the late-thirteenth-century font.

26. Chedworth

A quite large scattered village spread along a valley, with its church and cottages perched on the steep slopes, Chedworth has a number of pretty seventeenth and eighteen houses and a well-regarded public house, the Seven Tuns Inn, said to date to 1610. Opposite the inn, at the middle of the village, a large stone trough is fed by water that cascades from a stream above.

The oldest part of the twelfth-century Norman Church of St Andrew is its large embattled tower of around 1100, although its top stage is thirteenth century. The building's fine Perpendicular south wall was rebuilt in 1461 by a Richard Sly – probably a wealthy wool merchant. Other notable Perpendicular work is the south doorway, dated 1491, and the glorious south range of five windows. Also of interest are the early Norman tub font, the elegant stone Perpendicular pulpit and a marvellous modern sculpture of the Virgin and Child, created by Helen Rock in 1911.

Many people who visit Chedworth, however, come not to see the village itself, but to see what must rank among the country's most beautifully sited Roman villas. It was discovered quite by accident in 1864, when Lord Eldon's gamekeeper – digging to recover a ferret lost in a rabbit hole in the middle of Chedworth Woods – began finding bits of tessellated paving. A subsequent excavation revealed a substantial Roman villa that dates from around AD 120 to AD 400 and includes a number of beautiful mosaic pavements, as well as bath suites and a hypocaust. The first structure at the villa dates to the second century AD. This was improved and extended over the following couple of centuries, reaching its heyday in the fourth century AD, during which time it was a place of wealth and luxury. It fell into disrepair and ruin,

Hypocaust heating system at Chedworth Roman Villa.

however, around the time the Roman Empire left Britain in AD 410. When the villa was excavated local stone was placed on top of the surviving walls to reconstruct the outline of the buildings. Chedworth Roman Villa has been in the care of the National Trust since 1924. There is a café and museum at the site. (Further information is available online at www.nationaltrust.org.uk/chedworth-roman-villa.)

Severn Vale

27. Gloucester Cathedral

Whether approaching Gloucester from the Cotswolds or from the Severn Vale, the city's spectacular cathedral, with its colossal central tower, is visible from miles around. The best view of the building when approaching on foot is seen from College Street, where it opens onto College Green, or from beneath the thirteenth-century archway of St Mary's Gate, off St Mary's Square. The pinnacle-topped tower, constructed in the 1450s and reaching up to a height of 225 feet, is sensational.

An Anglo-Saxon prince named Osric founded a religious house on the cathedral site around 679. This came under Benedictine rule around 1016, and then, following the Norman Conquest, William I appointed an associate, Serlo, as abbot of the monastery in 1072. By this time, though, it was in decline, with just two monks and eight novices. A major fire that ravaged much of the immediate area in 1088 is thought to have destroyed most of the Saxon building and in the following year Serlo laid the foundation stone of a new building, much of which survives. Known as the Abbey of St Peter, it was, however, severely damaged by fire in 1122.

Further building continued in the twelfth century and in 1216 Henry III was crowned king in the abbey church. Over a century later, on 21 September 1327, Edward II met his death while imprisoned at Berkeley Castle. His body was brought to Gloucester, where he was buried in the abbey, with a majestic shrine-like monument being erected over his tomb. Situated in the north ambulatory, an alabaster effigy of the king rests on the tomb chest, which is clad in marble and surrounded by an ornately carved canopy of limestone pillars and arches. Considerable sums of money were subsequently raised by the many pilgrims who visited the tomb. The entire structure is a work of breathtaking craftsmanship.

Other inspiring fourteenth-century features in the abbey include the cloisters, with their superb fan vaulting – as seen in the series of *Harry Potter* movies – and the Great East Window. This is situated in the quire behind the high altar and covers the entire east end of the building. Installed in the early 1350s, the window is a landmark of English medieval glass. The abbey became Gloucester Cathedral in 1541, and then, during the Civil War, there were plans for its total destruction. Mercifully, a reprieve was granted to the mayor and corporation in 1656.

Above: Gloucester Cathedral's tower glimpsed between the trees on College Green.

Below left: Edward II's tomb, Gloucester Cathedral.

Below right: The cloisters, Gloucester Cathedral.

28. Gloucester City

Gloucester has other fascinating locations well worth seeking out. A busy port in the 1800s, Gloucester Docks are nowadays a destination for visiting narrowboats and cruisers, rather than the cargo-carrying vessels of the Victorian era. Most of the original warehouses and buildings have survived, however, and are being used for other commercial purposes. Gloucester Quays, south of the main docks area, is a designer outlet centre. The imposing Llanthony Warehouse is home to Gloucester Waterways Museum, while several historic craft are moored at the quayside.

The ruins of St Oswald's Priory can be seen at Priory Road, near St Mary's Square. The priory church, initially dedicated to St Peter, was founded in the 880s or 890s by Lady Aethelflaed of Mercia, daughter of Alfred the Great. It was built from recycled Roman stones, although the ruins seen today are Norman work of the twelfth and thirteenth centuries. In 909, following a raid into Danish territory, the bones of St Oswald were taken from Bardney Abbey in Lincolnshire and placed in the priory at Gloucester, and the building was subsequently being rededicated to him. The priory was more or less destroyed, however, in the Civil War's Siege of Gloucester in 1643, leaving only the existing ruins. A fragment of a ninth-century Anglo-Saxon cross shaft discovered by archaeologists working on the site in the 1970s can be seen in Gloucester City Museum.

Hillfield Gardens, off the London Road and just outside the city centre, were originally the grounds of the elaborate Victorian Hillfield House. Open to the public, these secluded gardens are home to three curious and interesting monuments,

Warehouses at Gloucester Docks.

including the disused chapel of the former leper hospital of St Mary Magdalene. The chapel was abandoned in the 1840s and the nave pulled down in 1861, the surviving late twelfth-century chancel – which contains a recumbent effigy from around 1290 – being entered through a doorway in the blocked chancel arch. The Norman north and south doorways of St Mary Magdalene's demolished nave have been preserved, with the more elaborate of the two set against the chancel arch.

Also in the gardens is a small decagonal fourteenth-century building, its front half open with an arcade of five arches. Known as The King's Board, it originally stood at Westgate Street, possibly as a preaching cross, although by the 1580s it was used as a butter market. In 1693, with its roof taken down, its top was converted to a cistern for the storage of water, the structure being brought to its present location in 1937.

The last of the three monuments is an elaborately carved open octagonal stone structure called Scriven's Conduit. Put up at Southgate Street in 1636 to channel water to the city, it remained there until 1784, being moved to Hillfield Gardens in 1937. Its top, thought to have been rebuilt in 1705, supports a weathered finial carrying a statue of Jupiter Fluvius – the giver of rain in Roman mythology – pouring rainwater onto Sabrina, the Welsh goddess of the River Severn.

St Oswald's Priory ruin, Gloucester.

The King's Board at Gloucester's Hillfield Gardens.

29. Saul

The village of Saul, around 9 miles south-west of Gloucester, is where the Gloucester and Sharpness Canal crosses the line of the earlier Stroudwater Canal. Opened in 1827, the Gloucester and Sharpness Canal is 16.5 miles long and was once the broadest and deepest ship canal in the world. The principal reason for its construction was to allow shipping, which was heading for Gloucester docks, to avoid a winding and treacherous stretch of the River Severn. At its opening, the canal could take craft up to 600 tons in weight, with a wide range of cargoes being carried. In 1960 an oil depot was opened beside a wharf at Quedgeley, bulk oil carriers thus adding to the vessels using the waterway. Indeed, in 1937 two Royal Navy submarines navigated the canal.

Earlier, the Stroudwater Canal – properly called the Stroudwater Navigation – had been opened in 1779, linking the River Severn at nearby Framilode with Stroud, thereby enabling a supply of coal to the Stroud woollen trade. Competition from the Stonehouse & Nailsworth Railway, however, helped to bring about a decline in the canal's fortunes and it was formally abandoned in 1954.

For those who appreciate inland waterways, there is much to enjoy at Saul. Saul Junction, with its air of unhurried activity, is the point where the Gloucester and Sharpness Canal crosses the line of the Stroudwater Canal. The house at the junction was built for the official who would collect tolls from vessels passing from one canal to the other and open the bridge over the Gloucester Canal. Junction Lock is a fine unaltered lock dated 1826, which can be seen at the beginning of the derelict arm of the Stroudwater Canal. This was used to raise the level of the Stroudwater Canal by around 4 feet to suit the level of the Gloucester Canal.

Nearby is a heritage centre established by the Cotswold Canals Trust, from where boat trips for the public are operated at weekends. A little to the south of the junction is the 284-berth Saul Marina, which was completed in 2008.

Saul Junction, with Junction Lock in the foreground.

30. Slimbridge

Situated around 12 miles south-west of Gloucester, Slimbridge is probably best known for its famous wildfowl reserve. The Wildfowl and Wetlands Trust is a reserve occupying some 120 acres, attracting large flocks of ducks, geese and swans. Opened in 1946 by artist and naturalist Sir Peter Scott – the son of Antarctic explorer Robert Scott – the centre offers access to a huge variety of wildfowl. The centre's Sloane Observation Tower provides views towards the Cotswold escarpment, River Severn and Forest of Dean.

There are, however, other interesting features in the village. The Church of St John, which has a bold tower, topped with pinnacles and surmounted by a tall steeple, dates to the thirteenth century and is regarded as one of the county's best examples of the period's Early Gothic style. The capitals in the inner porch of the south doorway display early thirteenth-century foliage carving of exceptional quality and beauty. Outside, there is a good selection of chest tombs along the south side of the church. One, immediately south-east of the porch, is dated to around 1710 and is delicately carved with figures that include trumpeting cherubs. Occupying ground immediately north-east of the churchyard and close to the vicarage is a water-filled moat – said to be the site of a medieval manor house associated with the occupation of the rectory and church by Parliamentarian troops in the Civil War.

A swing bridge called Patch Bridge is reached if one follows a lane to the north-west. This allows the Gloucester and Sharpness Canal to be crossed, enabling access to the

Thirteenth-century carving at the Church of St John, Slimbridge.

Wildfowl and Wetlands Trust centre, which is situated between the canal and the River Severn. The Tudor Arms pub, close to the bridge, dates from the eighteenth century and was originally a beer and cider house for the Irish navvies who dug the canal. Patch Bridge and the pub are situated in Shepherd's Patch, a part of the village that developed in the nineteenth century, providing homes for canal workers and taking its name from the high ground on which sheep would be kept in times of flood.

31. Purton

The hamlet of Purton is situated on the banks of the River Severn, a little over 2 miles west of the Wildfowl and Wetlands Trust at Slimbridge – if one follows the Gloucester and Sharpness Canal, that is. It is, however, more than double that distance when one uses the road. From at least 1282 a ferry crossed the river from Purton to a village on the opposite side of the River Severn. Curiously, that village, too – which is near Blakeney in the Forest of Dean – is called Purton. The ferry, known as Purton Passage, operated until 1879, when it was replaced by the Severn Railway Bridge.

There are two swing bridges across the Gloucester and Sharpness Canal, which runs through the hamlet and closely hugs the banks of the River Severn. Close to the bridge opposite the Church of St John is a bridge keeper's lodge of the 1840s, with a pedimented porch and fluted Doric columns. The road over either of the two swing

The Gloucester and Sharpness Canal at Purton.

Above: Overlooking Purton Ships Graveyard beside the River Severn.

Below: Vessel run aground at Purton Ships Graveyard.

bridges leads towards the banks of the River Severn and to The Berkeley Arms, where a type 26 pillbox stands in the car park of the pub. Overlooking the river and with views towards the Forest of Dean on the far bank, it is typical of the defences built beside the River Severn in 1940.

Returning to the vicinity of the swing bridges, a towpath runs alongside the canal on the estuary side. Soon the River Severn is closely adjacent, and when the land between the river and the canal becomes a narrow strip, the 'Purton Ships Graveyard' becomes visible. From 1909 to the early 1970s a number of old vessels were run aground along the bank of the river to create a makeshift tidal erosion barrier, being towed from Sharpness docks on a high spring tide. The remains of more than thirty vessels have been identified lying in the 'graveyard', including the schooner *Katherine Ellen*, which was impounded in 1921 for running guns to the IRA. Some of them can be clearly seen on top of the bank – indeed, a number of them are visible on satellite mapping images – while others are seen protruding through the grass that grows on the riverside. These remnants are now under the protection of British Waterways and English Heritage.

32. Berkeley

Around 16 miles south-west of Gloucester and around a mile and a half inland from the River Severn, the small town of Berkeley is laid out to a plan that has changed little since medieval times. Berkeley Castle, with its great walls and buttresses, stands at the south end of the ridge upon which the town is situated, much of the fortress dating to the twelfth and fourteenth centuries. There is a great deal of interest to be seen, including the cell where in 1327 Edward II was imprisoned and probably murdered. Still lived in by the Berkeley family, the castle is the oldest building in the country to be inhabited by the same family who built it. A popular filming location, Berkeley Castle was used for scenes in BBC's *Wolf Hall* (2015), BBC children's drama series *The Ghost Hunter* (broadcast from 2000 to 2002) and the BBC television movie *The Other Boleyn Girl* (2003).

The thirteenth-century Church of St Mary, which stands in a wooded glade beside the castle, has among numerous features of interest a seventeenth-century detached church tower. This is thought to stand on the site of an earlier church. Especially notable inside the main church building are a collection of medieval wall paintings, including a fifteenth-century doom painting high above the chancel arch, while a twelfth-century Norman font is among the oldest of the church possessions. To the left of the high altar is the Jenner family vault where Dr Edward Jenner, pioneer of the smallpox vaccine, is interred with his father, who was vicar of Berkeley. To the south of the chancel there is a tablet monument to Edward Jenner.

Dr Jenner was born in Berkeley in 1749, and his ground-breaking vaccination work – initially opposed by religious figures and many in the medical profession – eventually led to the eradication of smallpox. It is claimed that his work has saved more lives than any other man who has lived and it is certainly difficult to overstate his importance in the development of the science of immunology. Dr Jenner's house

and garden now form part of a museum to his work and can be visited at Church
Lane in Berkeley. A particularly curious feature in the garden is Jenner's Temple of
Vaccinia – an eighteenth-century building under a thatched roof. He used this small
building as a surgery where, without charge, he vaccinated the poor of the district.
(Further information is available online at www.jennermuseum.com.)

Left: Berkeley Castle.

Below: Dr Jenner's
Temple of Vaccinia.

33. Over

The village of Over, situated on the busy A40 road some 2 miles west of Gloucester, is probably best known as the location of Thomas Telford's handsomely utilitarian stone bridge over the Severn, seen a short distance from the present road. It was completed by Telford in 1829, although not opened until 1832 owing to subsidence, and was until the opening of the Severn Bridge in 1966 the lowest point at which the river was crossed. It carried traffic on the A40 until superseded by a new road and bridge in 1975, since which time it has been used for pedestrian access only, being a popular vantage point from which to view the Severn Bore. The bridge gives access to the southern half of Alney Island, the large river island created by the parting of the River Severn into two channels, which rejoins near Maisemore after 2 miles.

This half of Alney Island is very prone to flooding and consists of flood meadows that provide habitat for many wading birds. A nature reserve has been created, which is managed by Gloucester City Council. There are footpaths and cycle paths covering parts of the island, with the nature reserve car park sited close to Gloucester's Westgate Bridge. The island is crossed by the A40 and A417 trunk roads, as well as the South Wales Railway from Gloucester to Cardiff.

Telford's bridge at Over.

Other points of interest at Over are to be seen on the opposite side of the road to Telford's bridge. In 1903 an isolation hospital was built on the site of Over Canal Basin at the Gloucester end of the Herefordshire and Gloucestershire Canal. The canal had been opened in two phases in 1798 and 1845, but, following the growth of the railway network, subsequently closed in 1881. The hospital closed in 1991 and in 1998 clearance work commenced, leading to the creation of Horseshoe Drive, Wood Mews and Canal Way. Alongside the housing work, however, the Herefordshire and Gloucestershire Canal Trust began excavating the basin, which had been filled-in when the hospital was built. In 2000 the reborn canal basin was completed, followed by the construction of the Wharf House and a short section of canal at Vineyard Hill, above Horseshoe Drive.

Beneath the hill to the north of Horseshoe Drive, the visible remains of a three-sided moat lie slightly south of the short section of twenty-first-century canal reconstruction. Low banks and undulations in the ground indicate where a mansion known as The Vineyard was built by one of the Gloucester abbots in the fourteenth century, later becoming the bishop's residence after the Dissolution of the Monasteries. In 1641 it was plundered by the Parliamentarians, subsequently being abandoned and torched in 1643. By 1647 the building was in ruin. Today this relatively little-known historical site is the best surviving earthwork connected with 1643's Siege of Gloucester.

The canal basin at Over.

34. Highnam

One of the first things to catch the eye when approaching Highnam, 3 miles north-west of Gloucester, is the strikingly prominent steeple of the village church. Although the tower and steeple reach a phenomenal 200 feet up to the sky, the interior of the building is no less dramatic, being an outstanding example of Victorian architectural and artistic achievement.

The name Thomas Gambier-Parry is virtually synonymous with Highnam. Having inherited great wealth following his family's ventures with the East India Company, he came to live at Highnam Court in 1837 and married two years later. His wife, Anna Maria, bore him six children, although only two of them lived beyond childhood. In addition to several notable philanthropic works at Highnam and Gloucester, Gambier-Parry had the Church of Holy Innocents created to the memory of his first wife and those of his children who had died prematurely. When the church was completed in 1851 its theme throughout was children.

The church stands on the Highnam Court estate and was the first major work of noted architect Henry Woodyer – a friend of Gambier-Parry's. Having studied the techniques of Italian fresco painters, Gambier-Parry painted a series of grand, ornate frescos in the church, and, consequently, the building is resplendent with colour. The Last Judgement is magnificently depicted over the chancel arch; in the north aisle Christ's entry into Jerusalem is shown; and in the nave Adam and Eve

Ornate fresco paintings in the Church of Holy Innocents, Highnam.

are seen leaving Eden. Additionally, all of the church furnishings are of the highest standard, with even the wrought-iron radiator grilles being impressively ornamental. Clearly, absolutely no expense was spared in the building of this beautiful Victorian church. The church is open to the public on various Sundays through the year. (Information is available on the church website: www.highnamchurch.org.)

Accessible from the A40 road and standing in parkland to the south-west of the church, Highnam Court was built of English bond brickwork in 1658. This replaced an earlier house that was badly damaged by the Parliamentarians after the Battle of Highnam in 1643. Following his acquisition of the property, Gambier-Parry laid out the gardens to a high standard, but following his death the gardens were neglected through much of the twentieth century. Since 1994, however, restoration has been undertaken and they are now returned to their former glory. They are open to the public on various occasions through the year. (Information is available at Highnam Court's website: www.highnamcourt.co.uk.)

35. Ashleworth

To the west of the River Severn, some 9 miles south-west of Tewkesbury, Ashleworth village is centred on ground to the north-west of the river and above the floodplain. It has a small village green with a fourteenth-century preaching cross that stood in the churchyard from 1886 until the 1970s.

The oldest part of the village is at Ashleworth Quay, where for years there was an ancient ferry crossing leading towards Sandhurst on the eastern side of the river. Finds at the quay, which closed in the 1950s, include first-century Roman pottery sherds. Close by is an unspoilt riverside pub, The Boat Inn. Although the existing building dates to around 1830, it is believed to have been preceded by a much earlier hostelry. Homely and traditional, it consists of a small bar with adjoining rooms, with outside tables and seating on the riverbank.

Ashleworth's substantial tithe barn, built in the late fifteenth century by the canons of St Augustine's, Bristol, stands a little to the north-west of the quay. In the care

Ashleworth tithe barn.

of the National Trust, it has two large gabled entrances, diagonal buttresses and a stone-tiled roof. Some 125 feet long and 25 feet wide, the barn has ten bays.

Slightly to the east of the barn is the Church of St Andrew and St Bartholomew, primarily of the twelfth and thirteenth centuries, although the interior north wall of the nave has Saxon herring-bone masonry, possibly of the eleventh century. Another particularly interesting and unusual feature of the church is to be found in the south aisle. Here, a boarded recess above the south chapel displays one of the earliest known examples of a royal coat of arms to be found in an English church. The richly painted Tudor arms, dating from the reign of either Edward VI or Elizabeth I, are supported by a lion and dragon, with roses and crown above. Also located in the south aisle is a fine seventeenth-century parish chest with heavy ironwork.

36. Norton

The parish of Norton consists of three hamlets: Norton (around 7 miles south-west of Tewkesbury), Prior's Norton (a mile north-east of Norton) and Bishop's Norton (half a mile north-west of Norton). The A38 Tewkesbury Road ran through Norton until 1932, but now bypasses it. Sometimes called Cold Elm Norton, the hamlet has a nineteenth-century brick-built school with a village hall next to it at its southern end, but most other buildings are relatively modern dwellings.

At nearby Prior's Norton, to the east of the A38 Tewkesbury Road, there is a small hilltop church that has a neat little tower with diagonal buttresses and amusing gargoyles – one of which is playing bagpipes. The church was severely restored in 1875–76, although the nave retains fourteenth-century features, especially the north

Wainlode Cliff beside the River Severn at Norton.

and south doorways. Norton Mill – a red-brick three-storey mill and mill house – was operating as a corn and grist mill in the 1820s and 1830s, but by 1910 no milling was going on there. The building stands close to the A38 Tewkesbury Road and River Chelt, slightly north of Prior's Norton.

Bishop's Norton, to the west, is centred on a roughly triangular green with a pond and has a couple of thatched cottages and some eighteenth-century farms and barns. A narrow lane leads to the north and descends Wainlode Hill towards the River Severn nearby, which swings in a curve. Apparently, there was once a ford across the river near this curve, which is supposed to be somewhat shallower at this point. In the nineteenth century a jetty existed on the riverbank outside The Red Lion Inn, being used for the unloading of coal from barges. The inn, with its imposing four-bay brick front, faces the river at the foot of the hill, and has a large garden area alongside the river. The riverbank in this vicinity has long been very popular with picnickers – old photographs showing the bank thronged with people.

The red marl Wainlode Cliff beside the south bank of the river a short distance west of the inn is a geological Site of Special Scientific Interest. The Triassic rock beds here are well known to fossil collectors, although it is a less popular site than Hock Cliff near Fretherne, being more overgrown and less washed by the tide. The cliff height is quite impressive.

37. Deerhurst

Around 4 miles south-west of Tewkesbury and close to the east bank of the River Severn, the fascinating and low-lying village of Deerhurst has long been subject to flooding. Deerhurst's name means a wooded area frequented by deer. There is a tradition that King Cnut of Denmark and King Edmund Ironside met in the vicinity of Naight Brook at Deerhurst in 1016, made peace and divided England between them.

The village is very unusual because it has two Saxon churches. The Church of St Mary is considered one of the largest and most complete Anglo-Saxon churches in the country. First recorded in AD 804, much of the church building seen today dates to the seventh and eight centuries, with Herringbone stonework in the lower half of the tower believed to be of the ninth century. High on the wall of the nave is an elaborate double triangular-headed window of the ninth or tenth century and in the west porch there is a remarkable carving of the Virgin with Child. Dated to the ninth or tenth century, this carving would originally have been painted. Of particular interest in the north-west corner of the church is a ninth-century font, which, until its discovery in the nineteenth century, had been used as a horse trough at a local farm. There is a thirteenth-century stone coffin with a fine lid at the east end of the north aisle, while a brass to Sir John Cassey (d. 1400) and his wife, Alice, is very unusual in that her feet rest on a dog inscribed with its name, Terri. The only other known memorial with a named pet dog is at Ingham, Norfolk. A beast's head sculpture above the west door is traditionally associated with a serpent that was said to have been carried up the River Severn and to have ravaged the area until it was dealt a fatal blow with an axe wielded by a local man named John Smith.

Above: The Anglo-Saxon Church of
St Mary, Deerhurst.

Right: Ninth-century font in the church
at Deerhurst.

A couple of hundred yards south-east of the church, forming part of the seventeenth-century Abbot's Court, is one of England's most complete surviving late Saxon churches. Odda's Chapel was found in 1885 when repairs were being undertaken at Abbot's Court, the Saxon building finally being properly repaired and restored in 1965. Most unusually, the building can be dated precisely to 1056, owing to the discovery of a large stone found nearby in 1675. The stone (now in Oxford's Ashmolean Museum) bears an inscription that describes how Earl Odda ordered the chapel to be built on 12 April 1056. The building consists of a rectangular nave and a smaller chancel, the main Saxon features being the alternating long and short quoins, the windows, the chancel arch and the north door of the nave.

38. Tewkesbury

Close to the confluence of the River Severn and River Avon, the appealing town of Tewkesbury is chiefly medieval in origin, as evidenced by the numerous timber-framed buildings that survive from the fifteenth to seventeenth centuries. Dominating the town, however, is the cathedral-like Abbey Church of St Mary, which was saved from destruction during the Dissolution of the Monasteries when the townspeople bought it for £453 for use as their parish church. An outstanding expression of Norman power, its massive tower – the largest Norman church tower in existence – is a landmark for miles around. Founded in 1087, much of the building had been completed by the early 1120s, although the tower was not finished until nearer the mid-twelfth century. Standing 65 feet high and seven times recessed, the abbey's colossal west front is especially striking. Possibly the most awe-inspiring sight that catches the eye as one enters the nave is the enormous piers and vaulted roof. The fourteenth-century stained glass in the seven windows of the presbytery clerestory is justifiably famous.

The abbey has not, however, always been a scene of peace and serenity. A decisive battle in the fifteenth-century Wars of the Roses took place at Tewkesbury on 4 May 1471, when the Lancastrians engaged with the Yorkists on ground to the south of the abbey. Various factors led to the defeat of the Lancastrians, much of the resulting carnage occurring at the appropriately named Bloody Meadow, situated close to Lincoln Green Lane, a little to the south of the town and west of the A38 Gloucester Road. Many Lancastrian knights and nobles sought sanctuary in the abbey, but were dragged out, given perfunctory trials and executed.

Abbey Cottages, on the south side of the abbey, form an interesting curved terrace of timber-framed dwellings dated to the late fifteenth century. There are numerous interesting timber-framed buildings in the centre of the town, including the fifteenth-century Craik House in Church Street. Tewkesbury has a number of noteworthy pubs, too, including Church Street's seventeenth-century timber-framed Bell Hotel, which has a section of seventeenth-century wall painting preserved in the lounge, and the High Street's Tudor House Hotel, which probably dates to the sixteenth century and was subsequently enlarged and refaced in brick in 1701. Three storeys high, its interior features include panelled rooms and a fine eighteenth-century staircase.

Above: Tewkesbury Abbey.

Below: Craik House, Church Street, Tewkesbury.

Church Street,
Tewkesbury.

39. Forthampton

Situated 3 miles west of Tewkesbury and just south of the county boundary with
Worcestershire, Forthampton is a somewhat scattered settlement that stands on
rising ground above the floodplain of the River Severn. It has panoramic views over
the vale and there are numerous interesting buildings spread along Church Lane,
School Lane and Bishop's Walk, almost every one being a gem in itself.

Standing on the highest hillock, the Norman Church of St Mary, with its
substantially-buttressed fourteenth-century tower, was much restored in the nineteenth
century. Above the south doorway is a grotesque grinning Devil face, possibly of
Saxon origin, while of particular interest in the interior is the complete stone altar, set
on four chamfered stone supports. It dates to around 1300 and, as nearly all altars of
this kind were removed during the Reformation, is an unusual survival; indeed, it is
said to be one of only three pre-Reformation stone altars remaining in England in their
original position. The carved stone reredos behind the altar are by noted Victorian
architect William Burges (1827–81). There are several table tombs in the churchyard
and to the west of the porch there is a seventeenth-century sundial on a baluster.
Outside the churchyard gates are the eighteenth-century whipping post and stocks.

To the east of the church are the Grade II listed Yorke Almshouses of 1863–64.
An interesting row of four houses with tall outer gables, they have to their front a
timber-braced well head with an unusual gambrel roof. In Church Lane there are
several timber-framed cottages of the seventeenth to eighteenth centuries, while the
timber-framed Alcock's Farm at the end is even older, originating from the sixteenth
or seventeenth century. There are several buildings of note in School Lane, which
runs to the south-west, including Sanctuary Cottages, which are fine timber-framed
houses of around 1500, and mid-seventeenth-century Mill Hill Farm, which has
timber framing and two tall gables. Bishop's Walk is a lengthy lane that runs from
the village's western edge for a couple of miles to the River Severn and the site of a

Above: Vine Farm, Forthampton.

Right: Stone altar in the Church of St Mary, Forthampton.

former ferry crossing at Lower Lode. There are several buildings of note scattered along its length. The timber-framed Vine Farm, a Grade II listed building of the fifteenth century or earlier is particularly captivating.

The Lower Lode Inn, dating in part to the eighteenth century, is a popular riverside pub situated at the point where Bishop's Walk goes down to the edge of the River Severn. With views of Tewkesbury Abbey across the river and moorings for visiting boats, the pub is a comfortable place at which to stop and enjoy the gentle scene.

Forest of Dean

40. Newent

Situated on the northern edge of the Forest of Dean around 8 miles north-west of Gloucester, the quiet town of Newent stands a little to the south of the B4215 road. There is a great deal of interest in and around the town, which has a number of individual shops and businesses that make a welcome change from the chain stores one finds in so many town centres. In the Market Square there is a timber-framed market house that contains a single room approached by an outside stairway. This building, which stands around 10 feet above ground, is supported by twelve posts and was built around 1668.

A blue plaque at No. 1 Market Square, nearby, highlights the birthplace of record producer Joe Meek – best-known as the writer and producer of 1962 transatlantic chart-topping single *Telstar* by The Tornadoes. Things turned very sour in 1967, however, when he murdered his landlady, before fatally shooting himself. His black granite tombstone and grave can be seen in the town's cemetery at Watery Lane.

Nearby is St Mary's Church, which has a fourteenth-century tower with diagonal buttresses, battlements and a tall octagonal spire. The upper part of the spire has had to be rebuilt several times, the original spire having been blown down in a great storm of 1662. Bad weather caused further serious damage in 1673, when heavy snow caused the nave to collapse. The wooden ceiling of the rebuilt nave is said to be the largest unsupported wooden ceiling in the country. An Anglo-Saxon cross shaft in the south porch is believed to date to the ninth century.

Just beyond the church and close to the town centre, a large ornamental lake can be seen in the grounds of the former Newent Court (demolished around 1950). The lake, which is open to the public, was created from the fish ponds of medieval monks almost a thousand years ago. A well-maintained path surrounds the lake, offering an excellent setting for a leisurely stroll. There had been hopes that Newent would become a spa town, when in 1776 a local doctor, James Richardson, started prescribing mineral-impregnated waters from a spring at the east end of the lake, and *Slatter's Directory* talked in 1844 of the town owing 'its principal consequence now

Above: The Market House, Newent.

Below: The lake at Newent.

to its spa and gardens'. This success was short-lived, though, and within fifteen years the spa was no longer being used. The lake, however, remains an attractive and peaceful hidden gem.

A major visitor attraction in Newent is the International Centre for Birds of Prey, which holds the largest collection of its kind in the world. Situated at Boulsdon House, just over a mile south of the town, it opened in 1967 with a small collection of birds of prey. The centre now has around seventy-five species represented by over 250 individual birds. (Further information is available online at www.icbp.org.)

41. Speech House

The Forest of Dean's imposing Speech House, which stands beside the B4226 road 3 miles north-east of Coleford, was built around 1670 as a hunting lodge for Charles II. The building served, too, as a court of speech where the Forest's laws were administered by important officials known as verderers – whose main role was to protect the trees, plants and animals of the Forest. To this day the verderers still meet there occasionally, although nowadays their role is mainly advisory and as an

Speech House, Coleford.

Above: 'Cathedral' window on the Sculpture Trail.

Below: The Upper Pond, Cannop.

intermediary between the public and the Forestry Commission. Traditionally at the centre of the Forest, the Speech House building has been a hotel since 1858. Today the courtroom – with its original panelled timber ceiling – is the hotel dining room, although it can be viewed by visitors.

There are a number of lovely walks and trails in the vicinity. The Cyril Hart Arboretum can be accessed from a Forestry Commission car park a couple of hundred yards east of Speech House. Established in 1915, with trees brought from China by Victorian botanist Ernest Wilson, it was originally called Speech House Arboretum, but was later renamed in honour of local man Cyril Hart, who dedicated a lifetime of service to forestry. More trees from around the world have been added over the years, with the collection now exceeding 200 specimens. A small lake can be seen to the south of Speech House and the arboretum. This was created in 1975 by damming a stream at the head of the Blackpool Brook valley.

A popular centre called Beechenhurst Lodge is situated a little under a mile to the south-west of Speech House. It has a café, picnic area, children's play area and a tower for climbing and abseiling, and is the starting point for the Sculpture Trail, where a series of sculptures inspired by different aspects of the Forest are interspersed along the route, blending into the woodland scene. A stained-glass window called 'cathedral' is suspended above the path, and measures 15 feet high and 10 feet across. An undoubted highlight, it was created by Kevin Atherton in 1986 and is situated near the woodland car park beside the B4226, slightly north-east of Speech House.

Cannop Ponds, another popular site near Speech House, are around a mile south-west. The two large ponds were created in the nineteenth century to provide water to power a very large waterwheel at nearby Parkend Ironworks, but became redundant when the works closed in 1877. Today they remain as an undisturbed and beautiful haven for wildlife, with a free car park just off the B4226 road affording access. There is a large grassed area and picnic site close to the ponds.

42. Staunton

Two and a half miles north-west of Coleford, the pretty village of Staunton is situated high above the River Wye, very near the border between England and Wales. Monmouth is just 2.5 miles downhill to the west, where the forest creeps down the steep slopes towards the river below.

The village has a number of notable stones; indeed, the first part of its name is believed to derive from 'rocky outcrop' or 'cliff'. The best-known of these is the Buckstone, which is a very large boulder of quartz conglomerate perched on a hill, from where a viewpoint provides a panorama of the Black Mountains in Wales. The stone is easily found by following a path uphill for a short distance at the south-western edge of the village. Once a rocking stone that could be moved on its pivotal axis with relative ease, it was in 1885 tipped off its perch by a group of touring actors from London, landing on the road beneath the hill and breaking into several pieces. At great expense, it was returned to the viewpoint and cemented together, an iron reinforcing rod holding it firmly in place.

Above: The Buckstone, Staunton.

Below: All Saints Church, Staunton.

A Forestry Commission track to the west of the village leads off the A4136 Monmouth road and runs through Highmeadow Woods, eventually reaching the River Wye. Along the track is a rugged and rocky cliff edge called Near Hearkening Rock, from where there are fine views towards Wales. One particular outcrop has a convex face, which apparently amplifies sound, enabling gamekeepers to hear the approach of poachers. It is said that the rock acquired its name from this curious characteristic.

Still more amazing is a massive boulder nearby, said to be the largest detached block of rock in Britain. The Suckstone is a huge mass of quartz conglomerate rock that may well have once formed part of the cliff face and became detached during glacial movement millions of years ago. Estimates of its weight have been many and varied, the most common suggesting that the stone weighs around 4,000 or 14,000 tons.

An ancient standing stone known as the Long Stone is the last of Staunton's significant stones. Standing 6 feet above the ground beside the A4136 road on the edge of Marian's Inclosure, at the south-eastern side of the village, it is a monolith of old red conglomerate. Believed to date to the Bronze Age, it is said to be at the central point of a number of ley lines.

The late twelfth-century All Saints Church is a sturdy little stone building with an embattled and pinnacled tower. Inside there is a fifteenth-century polygonal stone pulpit and two fonts – one is early Norman, the other is Perpendicular. Outside, the grave of pioneer metallurgist David Mushet is situated to the south-east of the chancel.

43. Clearwell

The village of Clearwell is at the edge of the Forest and only a couple of miles from the River Wye. A neat place with a large fourteenth-century cross at its centre, today the village is probably best known for its network of caves, which comprise a natural system of passages within the carboniferous limestone. Much iron ore mining occurred here, with subterranean workings thought to date in part from the fifteenth and sixteenth centuries, although earlier mining activity by the Romans undoubtedly took place in the caves. More than half a million tons of iron ore were extracted from the mines between 1832 and 1880, the last commercial raising of iron ore taking place in 1945.

Nine large caverns are open to the public, giving a clear impression of the scale of mining that took place here. On several occasions the caves have featured in episodes of BBC television's *Doctor Who* series, including 'The Christmas Invasion', 'The Satan Pit', 'The Time of Angels' and 'Flesh and Stone'. Folklore accounts, too, have centred on the location, with a ghostly miner reportedly being seen here on more than one occasion.

An unusual attraction called the Secret Forest can be seen at Stockwood Scowles, 200 yards up the road from Clearwell Caves. This consists of an enchanting woodland, with a circular path weaving between gnarled and twisted trees, curious

Above: Chimney over the blacksmith's foundry at Clearwell Caves.

Below: Coloured stone in the chancel of the Church of St Peter, Clearwell.

hollows and peculiar rock formations. Known locally as scowles, this odd terrain is thought to be the remains of underground cave systems formed in the rock millions of years ago. Uplift and erosion over a further great timespan exposed these caves on the surface, iron ore gradually forming in the fissures and crevices. After the iron ore was subsequently exploited in mining activities, an already strange-looking landscape took on a positively bizarre appearance. The circular walk concludes at a replica Iron Age roundhouse settlement.

Clearwell has several buildings of note. The grandiose Church of St Peter, constructed of local red sandstone in 1863–64 to replace an earlier chapel of ease, has a tall steeple and a sumptuous interior with a mass of carving, coloured stone, brass, stained glass and an exquisite stencilled roof. Clearwell Castle, nearby, is a neo-Gothic stone folly that was built in 1727–28. Now a first-class wedding venue, it was used as a recording location by a number of major rock bands in the 1970s.

44. Parkend

Positioned at the foot of the Cannop Valley, around 4 miles south-west of Coleford, Parkend takes its name from its location at the north-eastern end of a medieval hunting park enclosure called Whitemead Park – now a camping and caravan park. The village was for centuries a significant industrial centre, at one time being known as the industrial heart of the Forest. A coke-fired furnace called Parkend Ironworks began operation in 1799, making up to 280 tons of iron at one point. A trade slump led to closure in 1877, however, and only the blowing engine house has survived. Today it houses the Dean Field Studies Centre, and although not open to the general public, this historically significant building can be seen from New Road in the centre of the village.

Coal mining, too, has been a significant industry at Parkend, most notably at the New Fancy Colliery, to the north-east of the village. It began around 1852, going on to produce some 500 tons of coal per day in 1906. By 1922 employee numbers reached almost 700 and New Fancy Colliery was among the largest and most productive coal mines in the area. Coal reserves became depleted, however, and the colliery closed in 1944. The site of the former colliery is now a Forestry Commission amenity site, the top of the mine's spoil heap having been developed as a viewing site, providing sweeping panoramas of the forest. It has become a popular bird-watching location, where buzzards, goshawks and ravens are commonly seen.

A striking sculpture known as the Miners' Memorial can be seen nearby. It consists of three 'arms' – the first is of Forest of Dean bedrock, the second of fabricated and pre-rusted steel, and the third of carved and blackened Forest oak – and was erected in 2005 to honour those killed or injured in the mines and quarries of the Forest of Dean. Also at the site is a Geomap illustrating both the geological landscape and the industrial history of the Forest of Dean. Some 900 square feet in size, the Geomap is flat and intended to be walked upon.

Of interest to steam railway enthusiasts, Parkend station is the terminus of a 4.5-mile-long heritage line that follows the course of the former Severn and Wye

Above: 'The Miners' Memorial', Parkend.

Below: Overlooking Nursery Pond at Nagshead Reserve, Parkend.

Railway to Lydney. The station was closed to passengers in 1929, but reopened in 2005. Finally, the RSPB's Nagshead reserve, which is a joint project with the Forestry Commission, is at the western edge of the village. It contains a wide mix of trees, providing habitat for a variety of woodland birds. Two hides overlooking ponds provide viewing opportunities, while an information centre, picnic area and two nature trails feature among the facilities available. Many might consider the reserve the very antithesis of Parkend's industrial past.

45. Brockweir

The pretty hamlet of Brockweir, around 8 miles south-west of Coleford, was once a busy centre for trade on the River Wye, being at the highest navigable point for larger vessels. It was a major boatbuilding centre, too, with vessels of up to 500 tons being built at sites near the riverside. There were originally four quays near the present bridge and it was a transhipment point from as early as the seventeenth century,

The restored quay, Brockweir.

with iron ore bound for Ireland being loaded onto vessels here. By the eighteenth and nineteenth centuries the quays were frequently visited by Severn trows – at more than 70 feet long, much larger than many boats using the river – bringing their cargoes up the Wye from Chepstow, 8 miles south. The merchandise would have been loaded onto barges and then taken on to destinations such as Monmouth, Ross and Hereford. The historic quay near the iron girder bridge was restored in 2009. Curiously, Brockweir is said to be named after Brieuc, the fifth-century Welsh saint from Ceredigion, who supposedly landed here.

The spectacular iron girder bridge across the River Wye – replacing a ferry that operated between the village and the Monmouthshire bank – was built in 1905–06 and is supported by two pairs of solid iron columns. In addition to this enormous structure Brockweir has several stone houses dating from the fifteenth to eighteenth centuries, and a rendered white Moravian Church of 1833, beautifully situated on the banks of the Wye.

A fairly recent addition to local gems is the Brockweir and Hewelsfield Village Shop and Café, a marvellous community enterprise staffed by local volunteers. Opened in 2004 by HRH the Prince of Wales, who described it as 'a triumph of community spirit', it is of traditional oak construction combined with sustainable technology and environmentally-friendly heating and electrical systems. It is in a superbly elevated location on the lane running uphill from the village centre and is much used by local residents and visitors.

46. Lancaut

Named after St Cewydd, a sixth-century Welsh saint, Lancaut is a deserted village within a bend of the River Wye and was originally part of the land left in Welsh hands when the line of Offa's Dyke was drawn. Ten households existed here in the early years of the fourteenth century, but by 1750 there were only two inhabited houses. Very little now remains, except Lancaut Farm, dating from the seventeenth to eighteenth century, and, close to the river below, the crumbling ruins of the twelfth-century Church of St James, possibly on the site of a seventh-century Welsh chapel. It was abandoned around 1865, and now only the roofless nave and chancel survive, with a double bellcote set beneath the west gable.

Some have claimed the nave is Celtic, but no evidence has been found to suggest the structure is any earlier than the twelfth century. The church's twelfth-century font was given to Gloucester Cathedral in 1940, where it can be seen in the Lady Chapel. Fine views of the limestone cliffs alongside the Wye can be enjoyed from the church, with the spectacular Wynd Cliff standing on the Welsh side of the river.

An exhilarating viewpoint known as Wintour's Leap is situated 200 feet above the River Wye on the B4228, close to the lane leading to Lancaut. In 1645, prominent Royalist Sir John Wintour made good his escape by boat after being cornered by Parliamentarians. Subsequently embellished, a legend endures that, on horseback, he leapt off the cliff edge into the river below – an extremely far-fetched scenario.

Above: Peregrine Falcon carving at Lancaut.

Below: Lancaut Church ruin and Wintour's Leap.

Gloucestershire Wildlife Trust manages two nature reserves at Lancaut. Lancaut reserve lies on the east bank of the Wye Gorge and is accessed from Lancaut Lane, roughly halfway between the B4228 road and Lancaut Farm. It is marked by a carved wooden peregrine falcon standing at the lane-side parking area. The reserve takes in several woods, disused quarries and limestone cliffs, consequently attracting a range of birds including raven, goshawk, sparrowhawk, peregrine falcon and kestrel. More than 350 plant species have been recorded at this important site. Wintour's Leap is part of the reserve. The nearby Ban-y-Gor Woods Nature Reserve, with its large ancient coppice and pollards carpeted with mosses and ferns, is described by Gloucestershire Wildlife Trust as a 'secluded and mystical habitat'.

47. Lydney

Situated beside the River Severn some 20 miles south-west of Gloucester, the small harbour town of Lydney is often overlooked but does have a number of noteworthy features. The harbour and its surrounding area is certainly one such feature, having in recent years become an increasingly popular visitor attraction.

Constructed primarily to transport goods and industrial materials to the port on the River Severn, Lydney Canal was opened in 1813. The harbour was completed

Lydney Harbour entrance.

Roman temple ruins at Lydney Park.

in 1821, and then extended in 1825. Both the harbour and canal remained busy waterways and transhipment points for many years until, after some years of inactivity, the harbour closed in 1977. The canal, however, remained in commercial use until the 1980s. Today the harbour is an interesting and peaceful historical relic, its pier providing views across the Severn to Sharpness Docks. On clear days the two Severn bridges can be seen in the distance, near the mouth of the estuary.

The Dean Forest Railway heritage line, which runs for 4.5 miles between Parkend and Lydney, has two stations in the town. Lydney Junction, around a mile north-west of the harbour, is conveniently close to the station on the main line between Gloucester and Chepstow, while Lydney Town station is central to the town and close to Bathurst Park.

The Church of St Mary the Virgin, to the south of Bathurst Park, dates from the thirteenth century and has a strikingly tall fourteenth-century tower and spire – rebuilt in 1897, following storm damage. Lydney's fine fourteenth-century town cross, on eight high steps, is at the north-west end of Church Road and is overlooked by the Town Hall, built in 1888–89. A rock-faced building with a large central gable, the hall's place in the annals of pop music was assured when the Beatles performed a concert here on 31 August 1962.

Lydney Park, to the west of the town, is without doubt Lydney's outstanding feature. A deer park created by the Bathurst family, it possesses the remains of a Romano-British temple built around AD 365, which is dedicated to the water god Nodens. The complex consisted of a basilica temple, now reduced to foundations, with a bath house and a large building with ranges of rooms around a central courtyard. It is believed the temple complex may have been more or less abandoned by the end of the fourth century. A number of effigies of dogs, associated with healing cults, were discovered during excavation of the site and these can be seen in a museum here. Lydney Park's gardens and Roman ruins are open to the public on selected days.

48. Blakeney

Situated at the confluence of the Blackpool and Soudley brooks, the village of Blakeney nestles in a wooded valley between Lydney and Newnham. Several round barrows indicate that the Blakeney area has been inhabited since at least the Bronze Age, and archaeological examination of a high-status Roman building, constructed around AD 75 and demolished towards the middle of the second century, revealed it may have been an early administration centre for a high-ranking official, possibly appointed to supervise mining and other industrial activities.

New Road leads north-west out of the village and into the heart of the Forest of Dean, passing through some particularly lovely scenery along the way. The Forestry Commission's picnic site at Wenchford, around a mile from Blakeney village, has picnic tables, a barbecue area and easy-access walking trails into the woodland. The pretty Blackpool Brook trickles through the site, where there is a children's paddling area, with a café and toilet facilities in the summer months. Unsurprisingly, this site is popular with families and children.

At Blackpool Bridge, a little further north, a stretch of the ancient Dean Road can be seen running alongside the modern-day road. The road, which ran from Lydney to Mitcheldean, is traditionally supposed to be Roman, although some have claimed it to be no older than seventeenth century. Whichever date is correct, it is certainly an authentic piece of early roadway. The nearby bridge originally carried the Forest of Dean Railway's mineral line over the road, but rail traffic on it ceased in 1949. An adjacent path along the trackbed of the former railway leads to Wenchford, while there are ample opportunities for walks in the nearby woodlands.

Mallards Pike Lake, around 1.5 miles further north-west, actually consists of one main lake, with a smaller one running into it on its northern edge. The site was constructed by the Forestry Commission as a boating, walking and bird-watching attraction, and as a forest beauty spot. It is fully accessible for buggies and wheelchairs, with the lower lake being used for leisure activities and the upper lake designated as a nature reserve. Also close to the site is the Go Ape tree-top adventure course. This consists of rope bridges, Tarzan swings and zip slides up to 35 feet above the ground.

Above: Forest trail along the track-bed of the Forest of Dean Railway at Wenchford, Blakeney.

Below: Mallards Pike Lake.

49. Soudley

Soudley, situated in a valley around 3 miles south of Cinderford, was once a busy industrial centre that had iron furnaces, railways and quarries in operation. Today, however, it is a lovely alpine-like village, popular with tourists and visitors wishing to learn about the area. An ideal place to begin is at the Dean Heritage Centre, which exists to protect and preserve the history and heritage of the Forest of Dean. Originally a corn mill, built on the Soudley Brook in 1876, it houses a museum describing the Forest's history and displaying a number of interesting artefacts, including an 1830s beam engine from Cinderford's former Lightmoor Colliery.

The forested area around the village is particularly beautiful, the man-made features and industrial remnants blending effectively into the woodland. Soudley Ponds are an excellent example of this. They consist of four man-made ponds that link successively through the narrow Sutton Valley. Surrounded by Douglas fir trees and in the care of the Forestry Commission, the ponds have been designated a Site

Dean Heritage Centre, Soudley.

Above: Soudley Ponds.

Below: Lane through the Forest at Soudley.

of Special Scientific Interest (SSSI), owing to the rich invertebrate population. They were formerly believed to have been created in the eighteenth century to provide water to the furnaces in the Soudley Valley, but this has been shown as inaccurate. The furnaces would actually have taken water from the Soudley Brook and from the mill pool outside what is now the Dean Heritage Centre. It is thought that Soudley Ponds – originally known as the Sutton Ponds – were acquired as fish ponds after the land was purchased by mine owner William Crawshay in 1836. Indeed, the lowest pond is still used by anglers of the Soudley Fishing Consortium, while the other three ponds form components of a nature reserve. They are surrounded by paths, accessible to wheelchairs and pushchairs, with footbridges affording access between each pond.

Probably of interest to hikers and those wishing to explore the hidden parts of the Forest is a route called the Blue Rock Trail. A 3-mile walk starting from an old railway cutting at Upper Soudley's Top Road, it follows a gravelled route that takes in the geological features of the Forest of Dean, as well as a number of former industrial sites such as Blue Rock Quarry, Shakemantle Quarry and – of particular interest – a ventilation furnace and chimney of the former Findall Iron Mine. Constructed around 1800 and extensively restored in the 1970s, it is the only almost complete iron mine chimney surviving in the Forest.

50. Newnham

The upper part of Newnham is perched on a cliff above the River Severn, and, until construction of flood defence schemes in the 1980s, possessed riverside sands that created something of a seaside impression. The prettiest village on the banks of the Lower Severn, it was once a relatively busy little port and was actually a borough town in the thirteenth century. In 1171 Henry II gathered part of his army here before setting off to conquer Ireland.

The village of Arlingham can be seen on the opposite bank. In 1802 a ferry regularly ran across to a landing point there, although this gradually went out of use after the Second World War. Shipbuilding was a significant local industry in the eighteenth century, and the town became an important transhipment point for the Forest of Dean. The few remains of Newnham Quay, which was in existence from at least 1775, can be seen close to the northern end of Church Road. There are easy walks along the banks of the Severn here.

Situated at the southern side of Newnham, the Church of St Peter stands on the end of a ridge above a red marl cliff known as Newnham Nab, its churchyard being a viewpoint with vistas across the River Severn and beyond to the Cotswolds. The building is mainly Victorian, but traces of the original twelfth-century fabric survive in the lower stages of the tower. The twelfth-century font is an important Norman survival, being one of a group of four – the others are in Hereford, Mitcheldean and Rendcomb.

Above: Riverside path at Newnham.

Below: View from the churchyard at Newnham Nab.

At the edge of the churchyard, above the river, is a charming and spiritually restful little enclosure called Newnham Peace Garden. In a secluded spot overlooking the Severn, it was created by the people of Newnham as a permanent memorial to those who died in the tragic events of 9/11.

A grassed area with embankments at an area called The Green, at the south of the village, is thought to be Civil War work of 1643, during which time Newnham was garrisoned by Royalist forces. The pleasant High Street, nearby, is on two levels and is divided down the centre by an open space containing a line of lime trees and benches. It has a mix of eighteenth- and nineteenth-century houses, with a tall, slim clock tower of 1875 in the central area. Among several seventeenth-century houses in the High Street, the Newnham Club was built in 1848–49 as a Town Hall and has a façade with Doric columns. Today it is a thriving community club. At Westbury-on-Severn, just over 2 miles north-east, the National Trust's Westbury Court Garden is one of the only surviving seventeenth-century Dutch water gardens in the UK.

Bibliography

Hart, Cyril, *The Industrial History of Dean* (David & Charles, 1971)

Herbert, N. M. (Ed), *Victoria History of the County of Gloucester* (Oxford University Press, 1996)

Mee, Arthur (Ed), *The King's England: Gloucestershire* (Hodder & Stoughton, 1938)

Verey, David & Brooks, Alan, *Gloucestershire 1: The Cotswolds* (Yale University Press, 2002)

Verey, David & Brooks, Alan, *Gloucestershire 2: The Vale and the Forest of Dean* (Yale University Press, 2002)

Walters, Brian, *Ancient Dean and the Wye Valley* (Thornhill Press, 1992)